The Writer Who Stayed

The Writer Who Stayed

WILLIAM ZINSSER

Foreword by Robert Wilson

PAUL DRY BOOKS
Philadelphia 2012

The essays in this book originated as "Zinsser on Friday," a weekly column published on the website of the *American Scholar* magazine. "Zinsser on Friday" won the 2012 National Magazine Award for Digital Commentary.

First Paul Dry Books Edition, 2012

Paul Dry Books, Inc.
Philadelphia, Pennsylvania
www.pauldrybooks.com

3 5 7 9 8 6 4 2

Printed in the United States of America

Library of Congress Cataloging-in-Publication Data
Zinsser, William Knowlton.
  The writer who stayed / William Zinsser ; foreword by Robert Wilson. — 1st Paul Dry Books ed.
     p. cm.
  ISBN 978-1-58988-080-1 (alk. paper)
1. English language—Rhetoric. 2. Exposition (Rhetoric)
3. Popular culture—United States. 4. Criticism. 5. Zinsser,
William Knowlton. I. Title.
  PS3576.I5625W75 2012
  814'.54—dc23
                                    2012031505

Contents

2 *Craft of Writing*

3 *Tech Age*

6 *Reverberations*

Foreword

IN DECEMBER OF 2009, the *American Scholar* published an excerpt from a speech by William Zinsser called "Writing English as a Second Language." We had been trying to encourage more readers to visit our website, and we thought that by offering a taste of the speech on the last page of the magazine and the whole text on the web, we might lure our print readers to our site. If we were lucky, they would find something else they liked there and perhaps return another day. Such are the modest stratagems of a magazine of modest means.

The ploy succeeded better than we could have hoped, and in one way we would not have dared to imagine. Many thousands of readers did find the speech, and because it was, like everything Bill Zinsser writes, lucid and engaging and wise, readers have continued to discover it by the thousands to this day. We didn't know at the time that Bill was not at first pleased to have been relegated to the web after having written for the *Scholar* and other print magazines and newspapers for decades. But his feelings changed when he heard how many readers were finding him in this new medium—many more, in truth, than would ever have read him in our print edition. Bill's new respect for the web led to the more remarkable way in which our plan had worked: he proposed writing an essay for our site *every week*.

Had I paused to deliberate before accepting this offer—manna from heaven—I might have worried that our first and, for the time being, only blogger would be eighty-seven years old, did not use email, and had never even read a blog. Instinct told me, though, that this was William Zinsser, for goodness sake, the man who wrote the book on writing well. How could we not say yes? Had I required further convincing, I might have reminded myself that earlier Zinsser pieces we had posted on the website after we had printed them had also drawn substantial and steady numbers of readers. (I suspected that teachers were assigning these web pieces to their classes.)

We asked Bill to write fifteen essays in advance, both so he would have a cushion and so he could see if this was something he really wanted to do, and we assigned Allen Freeman, a relatively youthful editor—two decades Bill's junior—to edit this first batch and shepherd the column as it moved forward. Soon after it began in the spring of 2010, Bill and Allen developed a low-tech weekly rhythm, with Bill's next essay arriving on a disc by overnight mail, Allen painstakingly editing it on a paper printout, and then the two of them discussing the edits over the landline phone, often for the better part of an hour, going over commas and word choices, the lead and the title, Allen ever patiently serving Bill's need to get each element of each essay just right. Sometimes Allen's patience would drive me impatiently from the office the two of us share—"Just get on with it," I'd think—but more often I would wonder at the lovely process unfolding within my hearing: two old-school guys confidently embracing a fresh new medium. Bill would write on the first anniversary of the column that he had wanted "to see if the personal essay, an old and honorable form, could find a place amid the clutter and chaos of the Internet."

We could not have been happier with the result, but after several months, Bill himself decided that what he was doing—mostly searching his own experience for anecdotes about living well or writing well—was not enough for this new form. He believed the essays needed to be more urgent, needed "to be alive in the present moment." Soon came essays related to the life of the city where he had been born and where he had lived much of his own long life. He found Manhattan's streets clogged with "Blackberry-toting multitaskers forever checking their tiny screen." He had a few unkind words for Tina Brown and other meddling editors. Bill was appropriately outraged when an audience at New York's 92nd Street Y, where Steve Martin was speaking about art, a subject dear to him, browbeat the actor into sharing movieland chitchat with them instead. Bill's fifteen-column head start had dwindled to nothing, and now he was responding to things in the culture as they happened.

Bill continued to perfect the column for the nineteen months he wrote it and stopped only when his vision deteriorated to a point where, he joked with Allen, his family began to worry he would fall into an open manhole while walking to his office. The best of the more than eighty columns he produced have been adapted for *The Writer Who Stayed* (again, with Allen Freeman's assistance).

We proudly nominated Bill for a National Magazine Award for digital commentary for the work he did during 2011, and were even prouder when he was named as one of the nominees. The competition was stiff—not only Tina Brown's *Daily Beast*, but David Remnick's *New*

Yorker and Jann Wenner's *Rolling Stone*. Bill and his wife, Caroline, joined me for the awards ceremony in New York in the spring of 2012. By then Bill was nearly blind. Because these were the digital awards, the room was filled with website producers and designers, the new generation of the digerati. When the award was announced, and Bill had won, I went to the podium to accept it. I babbled for a minute or two, as you do when the lights are too bright and the adrenaline is surging, and then I said that William Zinsser himself was there in the room, sitting at our table way in the back. The applause was spontaneous and sustained, a loud, long swell of admiration. Bill didn't need his eyesight to appreciate that.

Robert Wilson
Editor
The American Scholar

1

Culture and the Arts

Content Management

I'VE BEEN READING about a new app, called *The Atavist*, that will provide an online home for "long-form journalism"—articles that run more than 6,000 words and explore their subject in unusual depth. Now a dying species in the shrunken universe of print, those extended magazine pieces were once a bright ornament on the American literary landscape.

The godfather of the form, Joseph Mitchell, was a huge influence on journalists of my generation. I would study his seemingly effortless *New Yorker* pieces about old timers on the New York waterfront to figure out how such mosaic work was done. What I figured out was that only Joseph Mitchell could do it.

In the subsequent postwar era a new breed of buccaneering editors would blow Mitchell's tidy model wide open, creating a form called "the new journalism," in which writers often became actors in their own narrative and tended to mingle events that happened with events they thought might have happened.

At *Harper's*, Willie Morris ran at full length Norman Mailer's picaresque *Armies of the Night*, which featured, most conspicuously, Norman Mailer. At *Esquire*, Harold Hayes and Clay Felker turned Gay Talese and Tom Wolfe loose on vertiginous high-wire acts that are still remembered. Fifty years later, Talese's "Frank Sinatra Has a Cold" and Wolfe's "The Electric Kool-Aid Acid Test" are firmly lodged in college textbooks.

But since that golden age, with a few exceptions—notably including the *New Yorker* and *Rolling Stone*—long-form journalists have seen their market wither and have begun to look for a new home, the Web. It is for those orphans that the founders of The Atavist—three young guys in Brooklyn—have developed their new site. Their purpose is to enable writers not only to publish their articles at any length but to "enhance" them with videos, photographs, audio tapes, musical selections, and other digital supplements that will "deepen the reading experience." The three guys call it a "content-management system."

Content management. Isn't that what we used to call "writing"? I've been in the content-management business all my life. I look for content that interests or amuses me, and then I manage it into a narrative. It's what all writers do if they want to keep paying the bills. Dickens did it very well. So does every good crime writer: Arthur Conan Doyle, Agatha Christie, Raymond Chandler. Elmore Leonard was once asked how he keeps his novels moving so fast. He said, "I leave out the parts that people skip." That's content management.

As a teacher of writing I don't fret about the new technology. What worries me is the new terminology. In recent years I've tutored students at Columbia University's Graduate School of Journalism whose writing is disorganized almost beyond human help, but they seldom mention "writing" as what they came to the school to learn. They are here to study "new media," or "digital media," or "electronic journalism," or "videography," or some other glamorous new skill. Garbed in so much fancy labeling, they forget that journalism is just plain old content management. They return from a reporting assignment with a million notes and a million quotes and no idea what the story is *about.*

The reason, I assume—and I don't expect a Nobel Prize for this deduction—is that people now get their information mainly from random images on a screen and from random messages in their ears, and it no longer occurs to them that writing is linear and sequential; sentence B must follow sentence A. Every year student writing is a little more disheveled; I'm witnessing the slow death of logical thought. So is every English teacher in America.

"As a journalist," I tell my despairing students, "you are finally in the storytelling business." We all are. It's the oldest form of human communication, from the caveman to the crib, endlessly riveting. Goldilocks wakes up from her nap and sees three bears at the foot of her bed. What's that all about? What happens next? We want to know and we always will.

Writers! Never forget to tell us what's up with the bears. Manage that content.

Stardust Memories

IMMIGRANT LYRICISTS EMBRACED
AMERICAN LANGUAGE WITH FIERCE LOVE

As Time Goes By
Brother, Can You Spare a Dime?
Baby, It's Cold Outside
The Lady Is a Tramp
Everything's Coming Up Roses

THOSE ARE ONLY five of the dozens of phrases and idioms that have been added to America's vernacular speech by its popular songwriters. Traditionally, that's what a nation's poets are supposed to do. America had many great poets in the 20th century, and only Robert Frost, I think, left us any familiar quotations ("miles to go before I sleep"; "Something there is that doesn't love a wall"). As the poet Randall Jarrell once said, "Tomorrow morning some poet may, like Byron, wake up to find himself famous—for having written a novel, for having killed his wife; it will not be for having written a poem."

But all of you can think of many phrases that originated as song lyrics and that brighten your everyday life with their freshness and color. Most of them date from the golden age (1926–1966) of Broadway theater songs, movie songs, and popular standards, collectively known as the Great American Songbook. A later breed of troubadours (Bob Dylan, Paul Simon, the Beatles) would further enrich that heritage with vivid images and metaphors ("Blowin' in the Wind," "Bridge Over Troubled Water").

Here, to warm up your memory muscles, are another dozen specimens from the earlier age: "Accentuate the Positive," "Thanks for the Memory," "You're the Top," "Bewitched, Bothered and Bewildered," "Diamonds Are a Girl's Best Friend," "Someone to Watch Over Me," "She's Funny That Way," "I Only Have Eyes for You," "The Man That Got Away," "One for My Baby and One More for the Road," "High Hopes," "Let's Call the Whole Thing Off."

Unlike Johnny Mercer ("Blues in the Night"), a gent from Georgia, or Cole Porter ("I Get a Kick Out of You"), a WASP from Yale, most of the major songwriters were immigrant Jews from Europe, like Irving Berlin ("There's No Business Like Show Business"), or children of immigrant Jews, like Dorothy Fields ("I Can't Give You Anything But Love"), Ira Gershwin ("Long Ago and Far Away"), and E. Y. (Yip) Harburg ("Over the Rainbow"). They embraced the American language with fierce love. Irving Berlin is a miracle of linguistic assimilation. Born Israel Baline in Siberia and raised there until the age of five, he would write lyrics in his adopted language as intricate and urbane ("Puttin' on the Ritz," "Top Hat, White Tie and Tails") as any written by Cole Porter. (He also wrote the music.)

Ira Gershwin, George's older brother and lyricist, found his lyceum at New York's Townsend Harris High School, which had a required course in classical poetics. He also experimented with French verse forms such as the rondeau, the triolet, and the villanelle. His alphabetically adjacent classmate, Yip Harburg, was similarly addicted, and the two friends wrote a column of topical verse for the school newspaper, signed "Gersh and Yip," which they continued when they went on to City College in 1914.

But Ira's best advice came from a British playwright who said, "First learn your American slang." The vivacious musicals that Ira and George Gershwin wrote throughout the 1920s took much of their energy from Ira's Jazz Age coinages ("'S Wonderful"). "Oh, lady be good to me," he said, and "I've got a crush on you," and "Little wow, tell me now, how long has this been going on?" He said "I got rhythm," not "I've got rhythm."

One of the busiest of those immigrant scribes was Mitchell Parish, who wrote the lyrics for more than 600 songs, including "Stars Fell on Alabama" and, most famously, "Stardust," the most recorded popular song, with more than 1,300 versions in 40 languages. The words that

Parish fitted to Hoagy Carmichael's sinuous melody convey no information except that the song is about "stardust." He just threw in a carload of "poetic" words: *night, dreaming, reverie, love, kiss, garden wall, nightingale, fairy tale, paradise, roses, heart, memory.* But they don't add up to anything.

It's safe to guess that Mitchell Parish never saw a nightingale on the crowded blocks of New York's Lower East Side, where he was brought as a child from Lithuania, or a garden wall, or a rose climbing up that wall. He admitted that he never saw any stars—or, presumably, any of their "dust." Once, commenting on the paradox of so many astral bodies in his songs, Parish said, "Sometimes I think that those lyrics about the moon and the stars represented an escape. They expressed a longing for what I couldn't see."

I thought of Parish the other day when the great pop singer Margaret Whiting died. The daughter of the composer Richard Whiting ("My Ideal"), she was left without a mentor by his early death. Her father's occasional lyricist Johnny Mercer ("Hooray for Hollywood") assumed that role and guided Margaret's career. When she was 19 he urged her to record "Moonlight in Vermont," which, he thought, was perfectly suited to her voice.

"I've never been to Vermont," she said. "How can I sing a song about a place I've never been to? What is the significance of pebbles in a stream? What are ski tows?"

"I don't know, I'm from Savannah," Mercer said. "We'll use our imagination."

"Moonlight in Vermont" would be one of Margaret Whiting's biggest hits.

The Perils of Pauline Kael

ON NOT TAKING YOURSELF
SERIOUSLY AS A MOVIE CRITIC

MANY YARDSTICKS WOULD be needed to measure the number of inches devoted by the *New York Times* in the past few weeks to the beatification of Pauline Kael, the abrasive and highly influential film critic for the *New Yorker* from 1968 to 1991. The occasion for those retrospective rites is the publication of several books.

One is *Pauline Kael: A Life in the Dark*, a biography that recapitulates the career of a writer adored by her acolytes and loathed by her enemies for her combative demeanor and messy intellectual feuds. Reviewing it in the *Times*, Janet Maslin said, "Her love for film has no present-day counterpart, but neither does the brazenness" which reflects "the slugfest spirit of the times." Another book is *The Age of Movies: Selected Writings of Pauline Kael*, an anthology by the Library of America, which admirably collects in matching editions the works of America's literary giants. I'll admit that I was surprised to see two decades of film journalism canonized in the same church as Lincoln, Thoreau, Emerson, Walt Whitman, and Emily Dickinson; that's a fairly loose canon. But such is the fervor of this adulatory moment.

Reading the *Times*'s immensely long explications of the new books, I'm struck by how seriously all the players in Kael's orbit took themselves, whether they were actually reviewing films or just howling from the sidelines. They were *cineastes* endlessly squabbling over *ur-texts* and the *auteur* theory, critics pummeling each other with pugilistic glee. In one review Kael compared Robert Altman's *Nashville* to *Ulysses*, presumably Homer's. Her famous 1967 deconstruction of *Bonnie and Clyde*, arguing that it introduced a new aesthetic of violence in American popular culture, ran for 7,000 words in the *New Yorker*. Some were heard to suggest that the point could have been made more concisely. When the fever finally broke, Kael looked back on the shrunken universe that she had single-handedly spun out of her fierce love of the medium. "Remember how it was in the '60s and '70s," she asked, "when movies were hot and *we* were hot?"

I, too, was once a movie critic. As the *New York Herald Tribune*'s chief critic in the late 1950s, before *movies* became *film*, I reviewed more than 500 movies, many of them very good, and I don't recall that my fellow critics and I considered ourselves hot. *We* were not the story; the movies were the story. We were journalists who worked for New York's nine daily newspapers, the sole exception being Leo Mishkin, who reviewed movies for the *Racing Form*; he was its only provider of non-equine fare. We wrote for widely different constituencies, from the upscale *Times* and *Herald Tribune* to the downscale *Daily News* and *Mirror*, and we ourselves had little in common— though our paths crossed several times a week in smoky screening rooms—except the shared pride in our craft and a deep affection for the movies. It would never have occurred to us to write about each other.

It was the best of jobs in the best of worlds because people went about their work with enjoyment. I still run into old Hollywood press agents on the sidewalks of New York, and we fall on each other with remembered fondness and amusement. At that time Hollywood was still a small company town ruled by a half-dozen thuggish studio chiefs, who nevertheless made many wonderful movies that eased Americans through the Great Depression and World War II and helped the country to maintain its emotional balance.

My generation of movie critics, reared on those credulous films, acquiesced in their simple vision and can perhaps be blamed for perpetuating naïve "mainstream" and "middlebrow" values. But we always took the movies, if not ourselves, seriously.

Goodbye and Don't Come Back

MY PROBLEMS WITH POSTMODERNISM

I'M REALLY TIRED of the word *postmodern*. For 40 years it has been the pet plaything of critics who see a "postmodern sensibility" in every new cultural work. Its moment is long over, but I don't remember anyone telling it to go away. I hereby make that suggestion.

I doubt if I'm the only person who has never quite understood what *postmodern* means, or how long *post* is supposed to last; the word floats in a vast sea of postness. Seeking a definition, I looked it up on Wikipedia. It says:

> Postmodernism is a tendency in contemporary culture characterized by the problematization of objective truth and inherent suspicion towards global cultural narrative or meta-narrative.

That doesn't do it for me. Problematizationally, I have issues with it.

Next I asked some of my friends who are composers and artists. They helpfully took me back to the prior
movement called "modernism," which, they reminded
me, wasn't just a catchy label. It's an academic term, firmly
lodged in textbooks, specifying a period of revolutionary
change (1907–1970) that overthrew long-held Enlighten-
ment beliefs about rational and orderly thought.

The rebels came from many directions. "Modern"
writers (James Joyce, Gertrude Stein) broke the English language into seemingly capricious pieces. "Modern" composers (Stravinsky, Schönberg, Bartok) rejected
the traditional principles of Western harmony and tonal-
ity. "Modern" artists (Picasso, Duchamp, Matisse) and
the movements they sired (cubism, surrealism, Dada, ab-
straction) disavowed the literal representation of form and
figure. "Modern" architects (Gropius, Le Corbusier) re-
imagined what houses and office buildings could look like
and what materials they would be made of. Meanwhile,
Freud notified the "modern" artists that much of their in-
spiration came from an "unconscious" region that hadn't
been known to exist.

By the mid-1930s those radical modes of expression
were canonized in museums, art galleries, theaters, and
performance halls throughout the Western world; New
York got a new museum called the Museum of Modern
Art. The age of reason was dead. "Modernism" was here
to stay.

Except that it wasn't. In 1970 the historians who had
named "modernism" decided that it was no longer modern
and officially closed the door. So "postmodernism" was
born. The new torch-bearers turned out to be an owlish
lot. Unlike the giants of "modernism," who took the world

as they found it and worked solely from a personal vision, however freakish it might appear (Pollock, Cage), the "postmodern" tribe looked around and saw a world of fallible people, ripe for judgment. They adopted an attitude of superior insight ("We know how things *really* are"), better known as irony. Everything got an ironic spin. Everything had "edge."

The bitter musicals of Stephen Sondheim mocked the homely domestic verities of Oscar Hammerstein II. The filmmakers Joel and Ethan Coen gazed upon the American dream and found it hilariously "dark." Even the cartoons in the *New Yorker* took a sour turn, mean-spirited in their derision of well-meant hopes and intentions. I mostly stopped looking at them; cynical I can do without.

At heart, I think, "postmodern" was unkind. But nobody really cared because everyone was so clever. Everyone who mattered knew everything. Then came 9/11 and nobody knew anything. "Postmodern" ended on that September morning. There was nothing ironic about 9/11. Or about the never-ending wars it ignited in Iraq and Afghanistan. Or about the torture of political prisoners at Guantánamo Bay. It was a new planet and a new age. Post-ironic.

But look! Kindness is making a comeback. Sincerity has again become permissible. The Coen brothers' latest movie, *True Grit*, a sincere version of the old John Wayne heart-tugger, is their biggest box-office success. The television hit *Glee*, in which no edge had been detected, runs on one of the most sentimental formulas in showbiz ("Hey, kids, let's put on a show!"), its optimistic songs high on the charts. One of those songs says, "Don't Stop Believin'."

So I won't.

Blue Moons and
Buttermilk Skies

WHAT'S THE GOOD WORD TONIGHT?

TELEVISION HAS HIJACKED the weather and stolen its mystery. Poetic ruminations about the moon and the stars and the wind have no place in TV's world of scientific charts: runic arrangements of circles and arrows purporting to denote storm fronts, floods, blizzards, hurricanes, and other natural calamities heading our way. Radio is equally clinical. No pity softens the voice of the weatherperson notifying us that tomorrow's 96-degree day will have a "real-feel" temperature of 107.

Listening to those grim technicians during the summer's calamitous heat, I thought of an earlier breed of sky watchers who didn't take the weather so seriously. America's songwriters knew in their bones that the weather was not reducible to facts and figures. It's a state of mind, the stuff of dreams and yearnings.

To lyricists in the guileless 1920s and '30s the weather was a meteorological playground, and they didn't hesitate to write about phenomena not necessarily known to science: blue moons, paper moons, stardust, stars falling on Alabama, pennies from heaven, life over the rainbow, and love east of the sun. Rain, ordinarily a spoilsport, could be a lover's friend ("Isn't This a Lovely Day to be Caught in the Rain?"). Even the clouds cooperated. "What's the good word tonight? Are you gonna be mellow tonight?" Hoagy Carmichael asks in "Ole Buttermilk Sky," beseeching the sky to "keep a-brushing those clouds from sight" when the boy pops the question to his girl.

Still gazing heavenward, Carmichael explains in "Can't Get Indiana Off My Mind" that "the force that calls me back home, anywhere I chance to roam, is the moonlight on the Wabash that I left behind." Later he and that other country boy, Johnny Mercer, would write the ultimate hymn to summer weather: "In the Cool, Cool, Cool of the Evening."

But, beyond mere nostalgia, the weather served songwriters as a metaphor for a broken heart. In torch songs like "Here's That Rainy Day," mainly sung by women, bad weather was bad news, seemingly the end of the world. Of all those rueful ballads my own favorite is the one that has weather in its title. "Stormy Weather," by the composer Harold Arlen and the lyricist Ted Koehler, was the most famous of a string of hits the two men wrote in the early 1930s for the semiannual revues presented at Harlem's legendary Cotton Club. The first vocal recording of the song was made by Arlen himself, who was the son of a cantor and had a high, plaintive voice. Its huge success generated great anticipation when the Cotton Club announced that Ethel Waters would return to the stage— she had been mostly in retirement, grieving over a failed marriage—to introduce "Stormy Weather" in the *Cotton Club Parade* of 1933.

On opening night, late in the first act, Waters made her historic entrance. Arlen had marked the song "slow lament," and Waters sang it very softly, starting with the opening declaration, "Don't know why," and continuing in the same emotional color: "there's no sun up in the sky, / stormy weather / since my man and I ain't together / keeps rainin' all the time." By the end it was obvious to the mesmerized audience that she was singing the story of her life.

That kind of weather doesn't get recorded on any television chart.

~~~~~~~~~~~~~~~~~~~~~~~~~~~~~~~~~~~━━━

A Christmas Dinner

THE FROZEN WINTER OF 1944,
ON A BASE IN THE HEEL OF ITALY

LAST WEEK, on an archeological dig through some fragments of my past, I came upon a mimeographed sheet of paper. It was folded in half, and on the front flap, in typewritten letters pale with age, were the words:

THE 885TH BOMB SQD.
ENLISTED MEN'S MESS
WISHES YOU A VERY
MERRY CHRISTMAS

It was the menu for my 1944 Christmas dinner. I was an Army sergeant attached to an Air Force squadron that dropped supplies at night to partisans in Nazi-occupied Europe. We were stationed at a base in the heel of Italy, a region of desolate poverty. I don't remember that our life had any graces. We lived in tents, hunched against the frozen Italian winter, keeping warm with a makeshift stove that we ran on the same high-octane gas that fueled the bombers.

Yet someone had gone to the trouble of typing out a Christmas menu, arranging the appetizers and entrees and fixings in descending tiers, according to the conventions of restaurant typography. The first tier said:

FRUIT COCKTAIL
STUFFED CELERY   OLIVES

TURKEY SOUP	PICKLES
CROUTONS	GIBLET GRAVY

Next, in similar groupings, came Roast Turkey, Bread Dressing, Creamed Potatoes, Hot Rolls, Bread, Butter, String Beans, Cranberry Sauce, Marmalade, Coffee, Cream and Sugar, Pumpkin Pie, Mince Pie, Cookies, Oranges, Tangerines, and Fruit Punch.

Turning the page, I found another block of typing:

Alone of all American holidays, Christmas has been held inviolate, and will be observed throughout the Army by order of the War Department. By this wise exception men may have a brief respite from the grim business of war to restock their spiritual strength and reexamine their position in terms of the religion of their nation. This they may do with an untroubled conscience. They will reflect that the tenets preached by Him whose birthday is holy throughout the western world are sound, worth dying for, the very marrow of our culture. That some of these professed tenets may not be practiced for awhile is due to human failings and makes them not less true. They have been appraised in the perspective of time, they have survived many wars, and will survive this one.

With stout hearts, we see victory, if not near, certainly clearly in view. Then and only then we may resume our cherished habit of peace on earth and good will to all men.

Who wrote *that*? I wondered. Churchillian eloquence isn't ordinarily associated with the Pentagon. Whoever it was, I like to think that for a few moments, in that forsaken place so far from home, all of us—including non-Christians and non-believers—were comforted and nourished by his words.

Looking at that menu today, so many Christmases later, I think of all the places where young American men and women have since been sent—Korea, Vietnam, the Persian Gulf, Iraq, Afghanistan—to fight wars that were more ambiguous. Ours was the last "good" war; we never doubted that the Nazis and the Japanese had to be defeated. We saved the world and sailed through life secure in the gratitude of our countrymen.

In 1998 we were anointed "the greatest generation" by Tom Brokaw in his best-selling book, which coincided with the huge box-office success of Steven Spielberg's World War II movie *Saving Private Ryan*, about the heroic invasion of Normandy. The greatest generation never looked better. Then, suddenly, it didn't. Another World War II movie epic, *Flags of Our Fathers*, about the equally heroic battle of Iwo Jima, quickly withered away, and so did much of the popular interest in the greatest generation.

Well, that's, as they say, life. One day you're the greatest generation and the next day you're not. I'll admit that I enjoyed the ride—getting up every morning and thinking, "Hey, we're *numero uno*!" But I gladly accept our demotion to Generation Ex.

What I now think is that all of us who fight the nation's wars are one generation and we're all the greatest. Nobody has been any better than the men and women fighting and dying today in Iraq and Afghanistan. God bless us all. And wherever you are, on December 25, Merry Christmas!

No Second Act

JOHN HORNE BURNS AND *THE GALLERY*

THE AMERICAN WRITER John Horne Burns was one of those literary meteorites that hurtle across the sky and then burn up. Nobody remembers him today. But I'll never forget how his World War II novel *The Gallery* once intersected with my life.

In 1944 I was a 21-year-old Army private, formerly a sheltered son of the Eastern Establishment, newly deposited in Casablanca. I was in North Africa! *Me!* Nobody in my life had ever mentioned the Arabs. Our heritage was Europe; everything else was terra incognita.

The next day my fellow GIs and I were loaded onto a train of "forty-and-eights," decrepit wooden boxcars first used by the French army in World War I to carry 40 men or eight horses. Eight horses would have been more comfortable. For six days I sat in the open door of that boxcar with my legs hanging out over Morocco, Algeria, and Tunisia, a wide-eyed kid on a sensory high, intoxicated by new sights and sounds and smells. I loved the hubbub at the stations—Fez! Sidi Bel Abbes! Oujda!—and I romanticized the Arabs themselves, even the skinny kids with beautiful smiles who ran alongside our train and pestered us for C rations and cigarettes.

Soon enough I would understand that the Arabs weren't "picturesque." They were a severely deprived people, many with skin and eye diseases that modern medicine knew how to cure. It was the beginning of, if not wisdom, at least the knowledge that "abroad" is a complicated place, not reducible to travel-poster simplicities.

After six months in North Africa—the war itself had moved on—my unit was sent to Italy. The Naples that greeted our Liberty ship was a brutally bombed city, its docks wrenched out of shape, its buildings blown open, some of them revealing the wallpapered rooms of a former domestic life. Naples was the only port of supply and evacuation for the Allied campaign in Italy, which had stalled for eight months near Cassino with heavy casualties. Everything and everybody went in and out of Naples—exhausted troops on leave, wounded soldiers brought back to hospitals, and a company of predominantly black GIs who worked the docks.

After the war the first two big literary hits were novels of combat: Norman Mailer's *The Naked and the Dead* and Irwin Shaw's *The Young Lions*. But neither was *my* book for *my* war—the one that every returning serviceman hopes someone will write, catching in a mirror of familiarity his particular moment in some pocket of the larger war. Nobody was going to write that book for me.

Then, in 1948, somebody did. John Horne Burns's *The Gallery*, about an American soldier's coming of age in North Africa and Italy, was published to high critical praise. I hurried out to buy it and could hardly believe how many of the same streets the author and I had walked on—in Algiers, in Oran, in Naples—and how many of the same attitudes we shared. He even took my train ride across Africa on a "forty-and-eight." Burns, I learned, was a Harvard graduate with a Phi Beta Kappa key and a degree in English literature. After college he taught for six years at the Loomis School, in Connecticut, until he was called up by the Army.

The Gallery consists of alternating chapters called "Promenades" (Algiers, Oran, Casablanca) and "Portraits" (Hal, Momma, Giulia). All the men and women have some connection to the Galleria Umberto, a lofty arcade shaped like a cross that was the emotional heart of wartime Naples. Americans and Neapolitans came there at all hours to drink in its bars and shop in its shops and above all to buy and sell at black-market prices. Sex was one of the main items for sale.

To Burns, an Irish Catholic, the Galleria was rich in symbols. "Look at the design of this place—like a huge cross laid on the ground after the corpus is taken off the nails." Every character in his book symbolizes a type that Burns either loves or disapproves of. Louella, the Red Cross worker, represents American smugness. Momma, owner of the gay bar, represents Italian tolerance. Moe is the compassionate Jew, Maria the demure prostitute, Chaplain Bascom the hard-line Baptist.

The Americans were rich and the Italians were starving—that was the central degradation of the city. But who was more degraded: the Italians hustling to feed their families, or the GIs selling their cheaply bought PX goods at a huge profit? Burns fell in love with the despised "Eyeties" and "Ginzos" surviving with gallantry and grace, and hated the arrogance of American privilege and power. He thereby wrote the proto-Vietnam novel, anticipating by a generation the hubris that "the ugly American" would bring to another foreign land. Burns's loss of innocence is the book's persistent theme.

Riding high on his royalties from *The Gallery*, Burns quit his teaching job and wrote a novel called *Lucifer with a Book,* about a teacher in a school not unlike Loomis, which was attacked with a ferocity unusual even for critics lying in wait for second novels. He moved to Italy, wrote one more novel, *A Cry of Children,* which was also a failure, and drank himself to death in 1953 at the age of 36.

"He seemed to have lost some inner sense of self, gained in the war, lost in peace," his admirer Gore Vidal recalled in an essay he wrote about Burns. "Night after night he would stand at the Excelsior Hotel bar in Florence, drinking brandy, insulting imagined enemies and imagined friends, all the while complaining about what had been done to him by book reviewers. In those years one tried not to think of Burns; it was too bitter. The best of us all had taken the worst way." Like Burns, Vidal was a young writer who first came to attention with a World War II novel (*Williwaw*), as did Mailer and James A. Michener (*Tales of the South Pacific*). But each of those writers used his first novel as a launching pad, steadily expanding his interests to achieve a long and spacious career.

Recently I dusted off my copy of *The Gallery* to read it again. I was curious to know who Burns and I were in 1944. Revisited in 2011, *The Gallery* has the strength of its original vision and the weakness of the tendency of people in their 20s to think that their insights are uniquely sensitive. Fair enough: I know better than to reread the wartime letters I wrote home that are still in the shoebox where my mother saved them. I'm sure they are littered with rosy adjectives and sophomoric grand truths. But they were *my* grand truths, valid at that moment in my life, and I tried to keep that in mind as I again made the journey with Burns and found his book more ornate than I remembered. But at that age Burns's grand truths were no less valid than mine. We were two Ivy League naifs, soaking it all up, eager to believe that the world was still young.

I also saw—as I couldn't have known in 1948—that *The Gallery* anticipated three later classics of the World War II literature: Herman Wouk's *The Caine Mutiny*, Thomas Heggen's *Mister Roberts*, and Joseph Heller's *Catch-22*. Burns's psychopathic Major Motes is the ancestor of Wouk's Captain Queeg, of Heggen's Captain Morton, and of Heller's grand lunatics who keep Yossarian flying combat missions after he is entitled to go home. On a deeper level—compassion for the defeated—*The Gallery* laid a foundation for Norman Lewis's masterful *Naples '44*.

It was Burns's bad luck to write his best book first. Like Thomas Heggen, another early suicide, he lived with the growing knowledge that *The Gallery* was the product of a heightened moment in his life, the only one he was going to get.

Blondie and Dilbert

HOW CHIC YOUNG MADE ME
LOOK NONE TOO BRIGHT

THE NEW YEAR begins with a journalistic bombshell. As of January 2, 2011, Brenda Starr, Reporter, will do no more reporting; her syndicate announced that it is canceling the comic strip after 70 years. Seventy years! That's one of the great American streaks, no less impressive than Joe DiMaggio's.

As a literary form the comic strip is a textbook for any writer seeking the grail of simplicity. Every day, in four tiny squares, it tells a story that also embodies a truth we recognize from our own lives. In my case *Blondie* was that ideal narrative, the amiable companion of my childhood and middle years.

I first focused on its durability in the late 1960s, when I happened to read that Chic Young had written and drawn 14,500 daily and Sunday strips since the early 1930s. It was then running in 1,638 newspapers—500 more than its nearest rival—and reaching 60 million readers in 17 languages, including Urdu, so saturating the globe that it could hardly be sold anywhere else. The Dagwood sandwich was known in the heart of Africa.

But who was Chic Young? At that time I was writing for *Life*, and I decided to try to interview him. I began by looking him up in the magazine's files. Nothing! Not one article. I only found two small items stating that he had won a cartoonists' award. I managed to get his mailing address in Clearwater Beach, Florida, and wrote what I thought was a persuasive letter asking if I could visit him. He wrote back and said he'd rather not do an interview. I wrote again and asked if I could call him and further introduce myself. He sent me his telephone number and we talked for a while.

"Oh, Bill, it's just a comic strip," he said. But he finally agreed.

A large and gentle man in his late 60s greeted me at his Florida beachfront house. Before we did anything else he wanted me to meet his wife of 42 years, Athel, a former concert harpist from Rock Island, Illinois, and hear her play. As Chic Young and I sat peaceably on a sofa, enjoying the ripples of music, it struck me that my host was a man totally at home with the idea of home. Home was listening to Athel play the harp.

I asked him why *Blondie* was so durable. "Because it's simple," he said. "I keep Dagwood in a world that people are used to. He never does anything as special as playing golf, and the people who come to the door are just the people an average family has to deal with. The only regular neighbors are Herb and Tootsie Woodley. If a new neighbor came over with *his* problem, nobody would be interested."

He pointed out that *Blondie* is built on only four elements. "Two are things that everybody does—eat and sleep. The third is sex, which I can't use, so I substitute raising a family, and the fourth is trying to get money." The comic variants on those four themes have been as endless in the strip as they are in life. Dagwood's efforts to extract more money from Mr. Dithers find their perpetual counterweight in Blondie's efforts to spend it. "My real favorite, of all my strips," Young said, "is one that's beautifully simple." For example:

> BLONDIE: Dagwood, what's that bulge in your suit?
> DAGWOOD: It's my wallet.
> BLONDIE: Well, it looks very bad. (*Takes some bills out.*)
>   There, now it won't bulge so much.

"Someone might say, 'You're not going to dump *that* out in all those newspapers!'" Young told me. "But it's easy to read and easy to look at, and the philosophy is so basic." In only 22 words the strip compresses two fundamental truths: that a wife never thinks her husband looks quite right when he leaves the house, and that she never thinks she has enough money to run the house he is leaving.

Another Young favorite shows Blondie sorting the contents of her purse. Dagwood says, "Why do you keep all that junk? You don't use half of it." She says, "I know—but I never know which half I'm not going to use." A nice joke, but not such a scream that it pulls the strip out of shape. "I think up a lot of funny ideas that I reject," Young told me, "because they just wouldn't be something Blondie or Dagwood would say. Boy, you stick to your characters! You don't monkey!"

Chic Young died in 1973 at the age of 72. His son, Dean, who helped with the strip in his father's frail final years, took over the writing of *Blondie* and is still at it today. Speaking of great streaks.

I would hear from Chic Young one more time. On February 13, 1972, reading the color comics in my Sunday newspaper, I found Dagwood trying to give away two tickets to the new hit musical *Hello Henrietta*, which he won in an office raffle. Blondie can't make it ("My club is having elections tonight and I'm up for president"). Neither can Herb Woodley ("Sorry, Dagwood—the O'Neils are coming to play bridge") or Otis Finney ("My mother-in-law is coming over—I'd get killed if I went with you"). Another neighbor says, "Not a chance, Dagwood. This is our square dance night." Finally Dagwood says, "I'll try Bill Zinsser." The door is opened by a none-too-bright-looking fellow leaning on a crutch, his foot elaborately bandaged. "I can't go out with my sprained ankle, Dagwood," he explains. I took that as a high honor. Afterward, Dagwood runs into the kid Elmo. The final panel shows

Dagwood and Elmo walking down the aisle of the theater. "Some date!" Dagwood says.

The world of *Blondie* perfectly reflected the simpler America of a simpler time. That world is long gone, but Chic Young's formula is as old as Adam and Eve, and his strip has found its perfect successor in *Dilbert*, created in 1989 by Scott Adams, which now appears in 2,000 newspapers in 65 countries and 25 languages. Where in earlier decades the center of American life was the home, a closed universe with a familiar cast of characters facing familiar situations, today's American home is the office, an equally closed domicile where both Dad and Mom work until 8 P.M. with a family of men and women whose capabilities and crotchets they intimately know. Dilbert is Dagwood reincarnated in a hive of computer geeks micromanaged by the inevitably stupid Pointy-Haired Boss. Some things never change.

The Revenge of the Comic Novel

THE FINKLER QUESTION JOINS THE RANKS
OF MAN BOOKER PRIZE–WINNERS

I COULD HARDLY believe my retinas the other day when I saw that the 2010 winner of the Man Booker Prize was a comic novel—a comic novel!—called *The Finkler Question*, by Howard Jacobson. The award is given annually for the best novel by an author living in Great Britain, Ireland, or one of the Commonwealth nations, and Booker winners tend not to be a lighthearted lot. Since the first award in 1969, they have included V. S. Naipaul, Iris Murdoch,

Salman Rushdie, William Golding, J. M. Coetzee, Ruth Prawer Jhabvala, Ian McEwan, A. S. Byatt, Pat Barker, John Banville, and Anita Brookner, and their novels have left no acre of human misery untilled. How did Howard Jacobson and his comic novel sneak into that somber priesthood?

Bookerism is literature's hot parlor game. The judges are at least as eminent as the authors—one panel had both a Dame (Rebecca West) and a Lady (Antonia Fraser)—and in the weeks preceding their decision the English air is thick with envious speculation. The first nugget fed to the press is the "long list" of finalists. That list generates a flurry of gossip over who will make the coveted "short list" of five authors, one of whom will subsequently be announced as the winner, thereby making the shortest list of all. It is from the Booker people that the English language has been given a new verb, *to shortlist*, and authors so anointed are identified for the rest of their lives as having been shortlisted for the Booker Prize.

At the recent ceremony in London, Harold Jacobson "accepted the award to unusually enthusiastic and sustained applause," said the *New York Times*. The audience, I assume, was rejoicing in an event it thought it would never live to see: the liberation of the word *comic* from the label *unserious*.

"There is a fear of comedy in the novel today," Mr. Jacobson wrote in the *Guardian*. "We have created a false division between laughter and thought, between the exhilaration that the great novels offer when they are at their funniest, and whatever else it is we now think we want from literature." His award-winning book, *The Finkler Question*, was described by the *Times* as a novel about "friendship, wisdom and what it means to be Jewish."

What it means to be Jewish is a recurring theme in postwar American literature, and it has found its most poignant expression in comic novels. Bruce Jay Friedman's *Stern* and Philip Roth's *Portnoy's Complaint* are both deeply funny and deeply sad, and there's no instrument sensitive enough to register where one element ends and the other begins.

Every great comic work is serious in its intention. Joseph Heller's *Catch-22* is the World War II book that most closely captures the farce of daily military life, just as Stanley Kubrick's uproarious film *Dr. Strangelove* is the ultimate warning about nuclear rivalry. Kingsley Amis's *Lucky Jim*, the champ comic novel of our times, is far more than the sum of its laughs; in its wake the pomposity of British academic striving lies demolished.

When newspapermen talk about the great books of their trade they soon gravitate to an 80-year-old comic novel, Evelyn Waugh's *Scoop*. In 1930 Waugh went to Abyssinia to write a travel book about the grandiose coronation of the emperor Haile Selassie. There his reportorial efforts got bogged in a feudal 19th-century society, and his "travel" book, *They Were Still Dancing*, unwittingly foreshadowed what the newsreels would brutally tell us a few years later when the emperor's foot soldiers tried to resist Mussolini's invading tanks.

Waugh realized that the lens would need to be turned differently—mere reporting wouldn't do the job—and in 1933 he recycled his findings into the comic novel *Scoop*, in which a London newspaper mistakenly sends its bumbling nature correspondent to cover a similarly outlandish war in a small African nation.

Rereading *Scoop* today, I have no trouble recognizing my own country's latter-day military assaults on small

Asian and Middle Eastern nations whose cultural heritage it doesn't understand. Millions of honorable words have been written by brave journalists about the war in Iraq. But still untold is the larger American narrative of reckless lunacy and preening vainglory. When the great books about Iraq are written, I expect one of them to be a comic novel.

Singing Along with Mitch

MILLER REVIVED AN AMERICAN TRADITION

THE RECENT DEATH at age 99 of Mitch Miller, proprietor of the long-running television hit *Sing Along with Mitch*, took me back to a summer evening in 1991 at Chautauqua, the lakeside town in western New York that comes alive every summer—as it has since 1874—with a cornucopia of lectures, concerts, and other self-improving events. Lighter entertainment is allowed after sundown, and it was on one of those evenings that my wife and I found ourselves singing along with Mitch in Chautauqua's huge open-air auditorium. Densely seated among strangers, we were united by a tradition going back to 19th-century America: group singing on a summer night.

We had been given copies of the lyrics, but the songs were deeply familiar. We had sung them since childhood around a piano, around a campfire, on a beach, by a lake, in college dormitories, at Boy Scout camp and Girl Scout camp, in cars and buses, at Rotary and Kiwanis Club lunches, in American Legion halls, at church socials and

Grange socials and impromptu gatherings of friend and neighbors.

Some of the songs date from World War I ("Pack Up Your Troubles in Your Old Kit-Bag"). Some are about the land ("Home on the Range," "Carolina in the Morning"). Some are about work ("I've Been Working on the Railroad"). Some are spirituals ("Swing Low, Sweet Chariot"). But most of them are innocent declarations of love and longing: "Shine On, Harvest Moon (for me and my gal)," "A Bicycle Built for Two," "There's a Long, Long Trail a-Winding," "Till We Meet Again":

> Smile the while you kiss me sad adieu
> When the clouds roll by I'll come to you. . . .
> So wait and pray each night for me
> Till we meet again.

The melodies are remarkably beautiful, each one a simple line that leaves no doubt about where it's going, inevitable in its arc, instantly learned and never forgotten. Many are in three-quarter time, the most sentimental of tempos, an intravenous drip of yesteryear. One of them, "Let Me Call You Sweetheart," I was told by my wife, who grew up in the song-singing Midwest, has its own choreography, born of long custom. As the song begins, everyone puts an arm around the person sitting on either side and starts to sway with the music. Sure enough, when the first notes were struck, as if turned on by a switch, arms were deployed throughout the auditorium and the audience rocked gently to the lilt of the waltz.

Our host, the goateed Mitch Miller, was no TV talk-show pantaloon. A classically trained oboist and graduate of the Eastman School of Music, he began playing with symphony orchestras at the age of 16. In his subsequent career as a producer for Mercury Records and Columbia Records, he turned out to have a sure ear for vocal talent and a genius for packaging singers in catchy arrangements that would propel many of them—Rosemary Clooney, Tony Bennett, Johnny Mathis, Patti Page, Frankie Laine—to fame. He thereby shaped America's taste in popular song after World War II, before rock blew all the old conventions away.

At one point Miller also formed a quartet of male singers, and in 1958 he reluctantly agreed to try a sing-along format. The resulting *Sing Along with Mitch* made him a TV celebrity, and when the show finally ended he took it on the road for the older population that never lost its love of the old songs. Now, in 1991, at Chautauqua, he was still at it, and so were we.

A few weeks later I interviewed Miller in New York for a possible article. I wanted to ask him what qualities gave those songs their amazing durability. My article never got written, but my notes were still waiting for me this week in a tattered folder. (Note to nonfiction writers: never throw away a morsel of unused material.)

"Singing along has always been a staple of American life," Miller told me. "It's an oral tradition. When all the ethnic groups came over from Europe and they huddled together, one thing they had in common was singing: the German *Sängerbunds* and the Swedish choirs and especially the Italians, who were always breaking into song.

"All these songs have one thing in common: they don't throw you. They're within a range that people can handle. They're easy to remember because they build on the first phrase: 'There are smiles that make you happy, there are smiles that make you blue, there are smiles that et cetera.' Or 'Avalon.' It's nothing but a scale. The scale plants the tune in the unsophisticated memory."

Miller told me that he never used a bouncing ball on his TV show, as was once done in movie theaters, where a ball landed on every note to teach the audience how the tune went. "I only used the lyrics—it was the first captioned TV show," Miller said. "If people have the melody in their system, all they need is a reminder of the words. What audiences wanted from me was to be a metronome that would keep them in time."

At Chautauqua, as Miller led us metronomically back through the decades, it occurred to me that we were the last generation that would ever know and sing those songs. The postwar advent of television made us a nation of silent receivers, and since then digital technology has pushed us into deeper isolation. Today we sit alone with our computers, conducting our lives and our friendships without seeing anybody. Making music together is one of the pleasures that somehow got mislaid.

Thanks, Mitch, for keeping us connected.

On the Trail of Sublime

STARTING OUT AT NIAGARA FALLS

JULY IS WHEN America packs its kids into the car and goes looking for the sublime—even if nobody knows that's what they're looking for. I used to think "sublime" was a dumb word, a mushy rhyme found in every bad poem and bad song and bad hymn. But when I started writing about the great parks I learned that the word has a specific intellectual meaning.

I remember one July afternoon when I sat on a log in Yellowstone National Park, waiting for Old Faithful to go off. I had always assumed that the geyser erupts on a regular schedule—something like every 57 minutes. I should have known better. In Yellowstone, nature was still visibly at work, just below the surface. No geyser could be expected to be strictly punctual.

At the Old Faithful Inn, a rustic edifice that seemed to be made of giant Lincoln Logs, I saw a sign "predicting" the next eruption for 3:42—more than an hour away. It said that eruptions last anywhere from 1.5 minutes to 4 minutes, depending on shifts in the bubbling underworld, and can only be forecast one at a time. YOU TOO CAN PREDICT OLD FAITHFUL, said an adjacent mathematical table, which explained that in 1917 a ranger discovered "a correlation between the duration of an eruption and its subsequent interval."

Walking out to Old Faithful at 3:30, I found several hundred pilgrims already there. I was struck by the simplicity of what we were waiting for. Americans are generally thought to be unable to enjoy themselves without electronic help. At the ballpark a scoreboard or an organist tells us when to cheer; on television a laugh track tells us when to laugh; in cars and on walks a digital companion saves us the trouble of having to look at the scenery or listen to the birds or think our own thoughts. But in Yellowstone we were waiting for a show whose only component was hot water. There was no impatience in the crowd;

even small children seemed to know we had signed up for something you can't buy at the mall.

At 3:42 Old Faithful went off and everybody clapped. The eruption lasted only a few minutes, but it had a beauty that no photograph could convey, the water rising and falling and catching the sun and then slowly drifting off. Afterward, the motorized tourists went back to their cars and buses and the rest of us went back to the hotel. But the geyser continued to tug at us in the lobby and the dining room. Whenever its next predicted moment approached we all stopped what we were doing and hurried out to watch. My own fidelity was rewarded by several eruptions of unusual length and height, including one in which the dancing waters were silhouetted against the setting sun.

The idea of sublimity was first broached at another natural marvel, Niagara Falls, in the early 19th century. Until then nature had been regarded as the enemy, a hostile wilderness to be cleared and domesticated. How that notion began to crumble is documented by the historian Elizabeth McKinsey in *Niagara Falls: Icon of the American Sublime*. Tracing the theory of sublimity to mid-18th-century aestheticians—especially Edmund Burke's *Philosophical Enquiry into the Origin of our Ideas of the Sublime and the Beautiful*—Professor McKinsey says that the experience of early visitors to Niagara Falls called for a word that would go beyond mere awe and fear. *Sublime* was perfect. It denoted "a new capacity to appreciate the beauty and grandeur of potentially terrifying natural objects."

I decided to test that theory—when I visited Niagara myself—by taking a voyage to the base of the falls, as tourists have since 1846, on a boat called *The Maid of the Mist*.

As we approached the horseshoe-shaped Canadian falls, inconceivable amounts of water cascaded down around us. But our little vessel was undeterred: it kept heading into the cloud of mist at the heart of the horseshoe. How much farther were we going to go? The boat began to rock. I felt a twinge of fear.

Fortunately, in any group of Americans there will always be one non-sublimicist keeping watch. The man next to me, peering out of his hooded yellow slicker, told me he had been measuring our progress by the sides of the gorge and we weren't making any progress at all. Even with its engines at full strength *The Maid of the Mist* was barely holding its own. That was a sufficiently terrifying piece of news, and when the boat finally made a U-turn I didn't protest. A little sublime goes a long way.

In Bed by the Last Eight

MUSINGS ABOUT SONGS UPON THE
DEATH OF A FINE SINGER

THE CABARET SINGER Mary Cleere Haran, who died last month in a bicycle accident at the age of 58, was one of the brightest stars in a small galaxy of American preservation-ists—singers and singer-pianists who perform the classics of the Great American Songbook and are custodians of that literature. Their accompanying "patter" is a scholarly edifice, usually built around one of the great songwriters or a particular period in American popular culture.

A partial list of those hardworking historians would in-clude Karen Akers, Ann Hampton Callaway, Eric Comstock, Barbara Fasano, Michael Feinstein, Kathleen Landis, Andrea Marcovicci, Maureen McGovern, Daryl Sherman, and Ronny Whyte. Most of them have never known the luxury of a decent workplace: an adequate stage, a proper sound system, a landlord who doesn't treat them as just another item on the payroll. Wedged into a cramped nightclub or hotel lounge, they emerge into the spotlight as elegantly turned out as if they had the biggest dressing room in the world, not the smallest. Wedged into my own cramped seat in the audience, I watch them with admiration.

Mary Cleere Haran had a pure singing voice and a clarity of diction that didn't miss a syllable. Her quick intelligence and humor caught her affection for the social history of the songs she was singing. Except for Lorenz Hart, whose ballads of heartbreak she often sang, she thought that male lyricists were clueless in matters of romantic love. Oscar Hammerstein, she once said, told us what we "should feel," unlike Hart, who told us what we "did feel."

Only one lyricist, she believed, got it right about what the hormones were up to, and that was Dorothy Fields. Two of Fields's earliest hits, written with the composer Jimmy McHugh—"I Can't Give You Anything But Love, Baby" and "Don't Blame Me (for falling in love with you)"—were flat-out assertions of desire. Writing about Fields in the *Village Voice* in 1993, Haran says that Fields's persona in "Don't Blame Me" is "forthright and self-assured, making the lyric just about as sexy as it can be. Never coy. Never hesitant. She gets right to the heart of the matter, unlike some of the boys, who could be ponderous (Oscar Hammerstein), verbose (Howard Dietz), or flippant (Cole Porter). Which only reaffirms the age-old secret that men, not women, are the prudes in this society." Haran could also have cited Fields's "I'm in the Mood for Love," which proceeds from medium to full arousal ("But for tonight forget it! I'm in the mood for love") or "A Fine Romance," written with Jerome Kern for their great movie score *Swing Time*, in which Ginger Rogers complains to Fred Astaire that he won't nestle and won't wrestle.

Historically, the mother church of Tin Pan Alley was the Brill Building, on Broadway, where music publishers held court every day for songwriters demonstrating their latest tunes on a tinny piano. For those supplicants the publishers had only one piece of advice: "Get 'em in bed by the last eight." Meaning the last eight bars of music.

(Pedagogical note: 99 percent of American popular songs are 32 bars long—no more, no less. The Western ear has long been habituated to getting its narrative information in four segments of eight bars each. Only rarely has a composer felt that he needed more room to tell his story—most famously Cole Porter, whose "Begin the Beguine" runs to 104 bars. The beguine, once begun, never ends.)

In theory the last eight bars should build to a predestined conclusion, happy or sad, and bed was the publishers' destination of choice. But most lyricists didn't get anywhere near the sheets. Ira Gershwin specialized in love hoped-for ("Someday he'll come along, the man I love" or "There's a somebody I'm longing to see . . . someone to watch over me"). Cole Porter dealt in grand abstractions, preferably cosmic ("Night and day, you are the one. Only you beneath the moon and under the sun"). Oscar Hammerstein ducked into the subjunctive ("If I loved you") or the indirect ("People will say we're in love"). Many songwriters just left the job to nature: "Every little breeze seems to whisper Louise," "Skylark, have you anything to say to me?" Not much action there.

It took a savvy lyricist to slip around the codes of reticence. Frank Loesser managed it with "Baby, It's Cold Outside." In the final bars of that antiphonal duet the long-resisting girl finally agrees with her boyfriend that it really is too cold for her to go home.

The Writer Who Stayed

NOVELIST DANIEL FUCHS WENT WEST
AND WROTE SCREENPLAYS FOR 34 YEARS

IN "THE PERILS OF PAULINE KAEL" (page 9), I wrote about my stint as movie critic for the *New York Herald Tribune* in the 1960s, reviewing films that were largely a product of the Hollywood studio system. That column got me thinking further about those often-derided movies.

Many of the founding moguls in Hollywood's golden age were immigrants or the children of immigrants, uncertain of their cultural footing in the new world. To give their movies a touch of class they often hired well-known writers and playwrights from the Eastern literary establishment—near-celebrities like Dorothy Parker, F. Scott Fitzgerald, and William Faulkner—to write or rewrite a screenplay.

The sums offered were unimaginably large to the writers and playwrights, and they flocked to Los Angeles to grab the riches of Tinseltown. The moguls were ill rewarded for their largesse. When the scribes completed their assignment they toted their swag back home and thereafter seldom lost an opportunity to trash the studio chiefs for their philistine values and boorish ways.

One New York author transcended that churlish state of mind. Daniel Fuchs was a writer who had published three critically acclaimed novels while he was still in his 20s and had also sold stories to the *New Yorker*. But the novels didn't sell, and in 1937 Fuchs accepted a screen-writing job at RKO Pictures and stayed for 34 years. He found himself unexpectedly caught up in a community of dedicated craftsmen not unlike himself. Embracing that world, his novelist's eye and ear fine-tuned to the outsized dreams and vanities of its inhabitants, he would write one of the best of all books about the movie industry: *The Golden West: Hollywood Stories*.

"You get absorbed in the picture-making itself," Fuchs wrote. "It's a large-scale, generous art or occupation, and you're grateful to be part of it. What impressed me about the people on the set . . . was the intensity with which they worked. . . . They were artists [and] photographers, set designers, editors and others whose names you see on the credits. They worked with the assiduity and worry of artists, putting in the effort to secure the effect needed by the story, to go further than that and enhance the story, not mar it."

The Golden West was not conceived as a book. It was posthumously compiled from fictional stories—all recognizably true—that Fuchs wrote about his movie-writing years and was published in 2005 with an admiring intro-duction by John Updike. In his preface Updike can hardly contain himself from quoting passages by Fuchs that have an Updikean elegance of their own. I felt that I was watch-ing two thoroughbred horses on the final leg of a racetrack, each straining to outrun the other, every muscle fully stretched.

Fuchs [Updike writes] sees no shame in shaping a product for a mass audience; rather, he sees wizardry and a special kind of truth. "It had to have an opulence; or an urbanity; or a gaiety; a strength and assurance; a sense of life with its illimitable reach and promise." Fuchs finds good words to say about tyrants of the industry like Louis B. Mayer and Harry Cohn, men who, however misguided, lived for the movies, who demanded *the work*. "It was always surprising how underneath the outcries and confusion the work steadily went on. They never slackened; fighting the *malach ha-moves* [the Hebrew Angel of Death] and the dingy seepage of time, they beat away to the limits of their strength and endowments, striving to get it right, to run down the answers, to realize and secure the picture."

During my stint as a movie critic, Hollywood was an assembly line. All the studios kept under contract a platoon of stars and producers and directors who had to be employed 12 months a year to amortize their salaries. Inevitably, many of the 500-odd movies I reviewed were not very good, and some were terrible. But even the worst of them had been painstakingly manufactured. When I once toured the major studios I marveled as a small army of artisans and technicians fussed with infinite patience to assemble a jigsaw puzzle that would be correct in every last period detail. The most fatuous Virginia Mayo pirate movie got the same finicky attention that would have been given to *Gone With the Wind*. Today, when I think of Daniel Fuchs's book, I think of those men and women fondly.

2

Craft of Writing

Looking for a Model

WRITING IS LEARNED by imitation; we all need models. "I'd like to write like that," we think at various moments in our journey, mentioning an author whose style we want to emulate. But our best models may be men and women writing in fields different from our own. When I wrote *On Writing Well*, in 1974, I took as my model a book that had nothing to do with writing or the English language.

My earliest models were the sportswriters of the *New York Herald Tribune*, the *New York Times*, and the baseball-obsessed *New York Sun*, an afternoon paper that I would yank out of my father's arm when he came home from work. I couldn't wait to read the latest insights of Will Wedge, who wrote three pieces every day under different bylines (my favorite was "By the Old Scout"), and of W. C. Heinz, who later achieved wide esteem as a magazine journalist and novelist. The sportswriters were my Faulkner and my Hemingway. They reared me on a style that was plain and direct but also warm. That style would last me well into my teens, when I discovered E. B. White.

White took the plain style and gave it urbanity. In his *New Yorker* essays he was a little more assured than the rest of us. He had a poet's ear for rhythm and cadence, and he had perfect pitch; he knew when it was O.K. to drop a slang term or a colloquial phrase into an elegant sentence without defiling its elegance. I saw him as a wise elder, talking to me with common sense and humor, and

I thought: "I could be a young wise elder!" I adopted that seemingly casual but hard-wrought style, and it carried me through two decades of writing for the style-proud *New York Herald Tribune* and for the best magazines of the day. I assumed I would write that way forever.

In 1970 I moved to Yale to teach nonfiction writing. During that period I did almost no writing myself, but I did a lot of thinking about how to help other people write warmly and well, and that process had nothing to do with handing down grand truths from an essayist's perch. It had to do with leading by the hand, building confidence, finding the real person inside the bundle of anxiety.

In the summer of 1974, when I was complaining to my wife that I was out of ideas, she said, "You ought to write a book about how to write." Her suggestion took me by surprise, but it felt right; I liked the thought of trying to capture my course in a book. But what kind of book? The dominant manual at that time was *The Elements of Style*, by E. B. White and William Strunk Jr., which was White's updating of the book that had most influenced *him*, written in 1919 by Strunk, his English professor at Cornell. My problem was that White was the writer who had most influenced *me*. How could I compete?

But when I analyzed White's book its terrors evaporated. I realized that it was essentially a book of pointers and admonitions: do this, don't do that. What it *didn't* teach was how to apply those principles to the various forms that nonfiction writing can take. That was what I taught in my class and it's what I would teach in my book. I wouldn't compete with *The Elements of Style*; I would complement it.

That decision gave me my pedagogical structure. It also freed me from my Svengali. I saw that I was long overdue to stop trying to write like E. B. White—and trying to *be* E. B. White, the sage essayist. Although I never met him, he and I were obviously not at all alike. White was a passive observer of events, withdrawn from the tumult, his world bounded by his office at the *New Yorker*, his apartment in mid-Manhattan, and his farm in Maine. I was a participant, a seeker of people and far places, of change and risk. Now I was also a teacher, stretched by every new student who came along. The personal voice of that teacher, not the voice of a classroom instructor, was the one I wanted narrating my book.

Such a book would require a different kind of model, written by someone whose company and turn of mind I enjoyed, whatever he or she was writing about. The book I chose was *American Popular Song: The Great Innovators, 1900–1950*, by the composer Alec Wilder. Wilder's book, which had just been published, was one I had been waiting for all my life—the bible that every collector hopes someone will write in the field of his addiction. I was an addict of the songs generically known as the Great American Songbook.

Wilder studied the sheet music of thousands of songs and selected 300 in which he felt that the composer—Jerome Kern, Harold Arlen, George Gershwin, Irving Berlin—had pushed the form into new terrain. In the book he provides the pertinent bars of music to illustrate his point or to single out a phrase that he finds original or somehow touching. But, beyond Wilder's erudition, what I loved most was his commitment to his enthusiasms, as if to say, "These are just one man's opinions—take 'em or leave 'em."

Thus I saw that I might write a book about writing that was just one man's opinions—take 'em or leave 'em. Like Wilder, I would illustrate my points with passages by my favorite nonfiction writers. Above all, I would treat the English language spaciously, not as a narrow universe of rules and regulations, talking to my readers directly ("you'll find," "don't forget") and taking them along on decisions I made during my own career as a journalist.

So it came about that I found my true style when I was in my mid-50s. Until then it more probably reflected the person I wanted to be perceived as—the youthful and witty columnist and critic. But that person was never really me. Not until I became a teacher and had no agenda except to be helpful did my style become integrated with my personality and my character.

Tips

I DON'T GIVE THEM TO WRITERS

"WE WANT YOU to come to our school and talk to our students about writing," said the voice on the phone, introducing himself as the chairman of the school's English department. I asked what he had in mind. "We'd like you to give our students some tips that will make them better writers," he said.

Tips! The ugly little word hung in the air, exuding its aroma of illicit information. Bookies live on tips delivered, horseplayers on tips received, investors on stock tips, preferably hot, and taxpayers on tips about how to evade the tax code. College-bound students pay for tips on how to ace the SAT test.

The tip is presumed to be based on inside knowledge, giving its recipient an edge in outwitting life's cruel odds, and never before has the tip-dispensing industry been so alive and well, plying us in magazines and books and on television programs with maxims of salvation. Golf tips (*keep your left arm straight*), tennis tips (*bend your knees*), cooking tips (*preheat the oven*), gardening tips (*buy a trowel*), parenting tips (*listen to your child*), sex tips (*take off your socks*).

"I don't do tips," I told the man calling from the school's English department. It's not that I don't have any; *On Writing Well* is full of what might be called *tips*. But that's not the point of the book. It's a book of craft principles that add up to what it means to be a writer.

Tips can make someone a better writer but not necessarily a good writer. That's a larger package—a matter of character. Golfing is more than keeping the left arm straight. Every good golfer is a complex engine that runs on ability, ego, determination, discipline, patience, confidence, and other qualities that are self-taught. So it is with writers and all creative artists. If their values are solid their work is likely to be solid.

In my own work I operate within a framework of Christian values, and the words that are important to me are religious words: *witness, pilgrimage, intention*. I think of intention as the writer's soul. Writers can write to affirm and to celebrate, or they can write to debunk and destroy; the choice is ours. Editors may want us to do destructive work to serve some agenda of their own, but nobody can make us write what we don't want to write. We get to keep intention.

I always write to affirm. I choose to write about people whose values I respect; my pleasure is to bear witness to their lives. Much of my writing has taken the form of a pilgrimage: to sacred places that represent the best of America, to writers and musicians who represent the best of their art. Tips didn't get them there.

The 300-Word Challenge

ON WRITING SHORT ESSAYS

I ONCE GOT A CALL from a woman who said she was the editor of a magazine called *Endless Vacations*. Endless vacations! The very name gave me a thrill: a vacation that never stopped. I could be seamlessly whisked from a safari in Kenya to a Club Med on the Riviera to a temple dance in Bali. When I calmed down I realized that what was endless was the number of vacations being recommended by the magazine, not the vacation itself. But I was hooked.

The editor explained that a regular feature of her magazine was a 300-word essay, on the back page, about an iconic American site. She had seen a review of my book *American Places*, a journey to 16 such sites, and she asked if I would write some 300-word icon pieces for her. I said that after two years of traveling and writing I was through with the icon business, but that she could buy any of my chapters and I would condense them into 300-word excerpts. I believe that anything can be cut to 300 words.

The editor agreed, and for a while we kept that gig going. After that she again asked if I would try writing a 300-word piece from scratch. By then I thought it might be an interesting exercise. I only insisted that the site be close to home; I didn't want to fly to San Francisco to write 300 words about the Golden Gate Bridge. The site I chose was Ellis Island, a mere subway and ferry ride away.

My only preparation was to arrange an interview with Ellis Island's superintendent; places are only places until they are given meaning by the people who look after them. I just spent a day walking around the site, taking as many notes as I would for a 5,000-word article. Nonfiction writers should always gather far more material than they will use, never knowing which morsel will later exactly serve their needs.

Here's Ellis Island in 300 words:

Of the two highly symbolic pieces of land in New York harbor, the more obvious icon is the Statue of Liberty; the lady embodies every immigrant's dream of America. But I'll take Ellis Island—that's an icon with its feet in reality. Almost half the people now living in America can trace their ancestry to the 12 million men and women and children who entered the country there. mainly between 1892 and 1924. "It's their Plymouth Rock," says M. Ann Belkov, superintendent of the National Park Service's Immigration Museum, which occupies the distinctive red brick building, now handsomely restored, where the immigrants were processed. "Tourists who come here are walking in their families' footsteps," Belkov told me. "Three of my four grandparents first stepped on land in the U.S.A. in this building."

Unlike most museums, which preserve the dead past, Ellis Island feels almost alive, or at least within reach of living memory. People we all know made history—American history and their own history—in the vast Registry Room, where as many as 5,000 newcomers a day were examined by officials and doctors and were served meals that contained strange and wonderful foods. Many had never seen a banana. "The white bread was like cake already," says one old man who came from Russia, his voice typical of the many oral recollections that animate the building, along with exhibits displaying the much-loved possessions that the immigrants brought from their own culture: clothes and linens and embroidery, ornaments and religious objects and musical instruments.

Strong faces stare out of innumerable photographs: men and women from every cranny of the world. The captions quote them eloquently on the poverty and persecution that impelled them to leave ("always there was the police") and on the unbelievable freedoms that awaited them here. One of them says, "It was as if God's great promise had been fulfilled."

Is there anything more about Ellis Island that an ordinary reader needs to know? The first paragraph is packed with necessary facts about the site: its setting and historical importance. It also contains an ideal summarizing metaphor ("It was their Plymouth Rock") and a tremendous fact about American possibility: in two generations the granddaughter of three of those immigrants had become superintendent of the place where they "first stepped on land in the U.S.A." The second paragraph fills the long-empty buildings with people—old-world men and women marveling at white bread and bananas—and with the belongings they couldn't bear to leave behind. The final paragraph tells what kind of people they were—what they looked and sounded like. It also explains why they left the oppression at home to seek a new life in America.

The language is highly compressed. Facts are crammed into one sentence that I would normally spread over three or four sentences, adding rhythm and grace and some agreeable details. But nothing fundamental has been lost; the grammar and the syntax are intact.

My students tell me that this 300-word piece is unusually helpful. They seem to be taken by surprise by its economy—that so much work can be accomplished just by tightening some screws. But the English language is endlessly supple. It will do anything you ask it to do, if you treat it well. Try it and see.

Detour Ahead

LOST WITH IAN FRAZIER

I AWAIT THE day when a Global Positioning System is developed for writers—a breed famously unsure of where they are and where they are trying to go. For a writer lost in the tangled wilderness of his narrative it would be comforting to just call Cheryl at GPS and ask, "Where the hell am I?"

CHERYL: You said you wanted to end with the scene where the grandmother forgives her children for pushing her down the stairs when she told them what was in the will. Do you still want to go there?

WRITER: Well, I've been doing some rewriting, and I think maybe it would be better to end with the scene where the family realizes they can't afford hip replacement surgery for the dog.

CHERYL: Hold on . . . I'm recalculating.

I like to imagine what would happen if Cheryl ever got hooked up with Ian Frazier, a writer of high impudence. Frazier is the king of detours. When I read one of his long nonfiction pieces in the *New Yorker*, I often find myself deflected into territory wholly unlike what has gone before, and I think, "How did we get *here*?" I once asked Frazier about this digressive tendency. I was editing a book called *Inventing the Truth: The Art and Craft of Memoir*, and he was one of nine authors who explain how they conceived and wrote their memoir. He had recently published *Family*, ostensibly a memoir about his Ohio parents, but before his journey ends he has trekked across vast regions of obscure early American history. This was Frazier's explanation:

> The artist Saul Steinberg once told me that I write fake boring books—books that you think would be boring, but then they're not. Faux boring. I tried to make this book sneakily interesting. I've always been willing to go in some off-the-wall direction—to drop everything and just run with it, where other writers might think, "I can't disrupt the fabric of my narrative." Ideally, each veer will make the narrative less boring.
>
> That tendency of mine is a direct result of bouncing off William Shawn when he was editor of *The New Yorker* and I was writing articles for him. It grew out of knowing what Shawn's threshold of boredom was. I would see his comments in the margins of my articles saying, "This is

neither funny nor interesting," and the section came out. My objective in dealing with Shawn was to tease him into keeping a section like that—to get him to say, "Well, it's neither funny nor interesting, but O.K." I've often found, when people have read one of my pieces, they will refer to something that was at first glance immaterial to the article. That was the one thing that stayed with them. Your objective is to find something that corresponds with the reader—something he or she has an affinity for, or can understand. It's a seduction. The reader thinks he knows what he wants, and if you can just tease him away from that he'll often have a better time than he would have had going where he thought he wanted to go.

Warning! I don't recommend Frazier's method; too much writing is already in enough disarray. You'll save yourself a heap of misery if you stick to the linear and the sequential, those twin pillars of good storytelling. But, hey, I also want you to live a little. Dare to treat yourself to an occasional crazy ride. Maybe it won't be so crazy. You never know.

"Who Would Care about *My* Story?"

SUCCESSFUL MEMOIRS ARE BUILT
FROM DETAILS THAT RING TRUE

EVERY SEPTEMBER they come out of the New York night—20 adults, mostly women, who have signed up for my course at the New School on writing memoir and family history. This is my 20th year of teaching the course, heading out into the night myself to meet my students and help them wrestle their life narrative onto paper. Most of them are paralyzed by the thought of writing a memoir. How can they possibly sort out the smothering clutter of the past? But mainly it's fear of writing about themselves. My suggested cure always comes down to two words: think small.

They don't want to think small. They are *writers*, novitiates in the literary enterprise, duty bound to obey its rhetorical rules and admonitions. I don't want them to think of themselves as writers. I want them to think of themselves as people—women who lead interesting lives and who also write, trusting their own humanity to tell plain stories about their thoughts and emotions. Why do they think they need permission to be themselves? "Who would care about *my* story?" they say. I would. I give them permission to write about the parts of their lives that they have always dismissed as unimportant.

One woman in my current class, in her late 60s, is from a prominent Christian family in Cairo. In 1953, when she was 10, the family left for America; her father, a former member of the cabinet of King Farouk, was out of favor with the new Nasser regime. They packed only their winter clothes, not wanting to reveal that they were leaving forever.

In America the girl from Cairo would have a long and successful career in broadcasting. But that really wasn't her story; thousands of immigrants before her had lived the same dream. *Her* story—the emotional core of her life—was the privileged girlhood in Cairo and the jagged rip that one day tore the whole fabric apart. I asked if she had ever written about those years; she deeply wanted to and was upset that she couldn't.

"I don't know enough about the political history of modern Egypt," she said. "I'd need to do a lot of research first." I told her she isn't Thomas L. Friedman and I'm glad she isn't. There is no shortage of pundits who will write sober books about the Nasser era, but none of them can write *her* story, and it won't need scholarly bolstering. If she just tells the story of one Egyptian family she will also tell the story of many other families under duress.

That idea had never occurred to her. Her gloom lifted. She was free! The following week she left me a brief manuscript called "A Fragment." Its sentences were dead simple:

> At last it's time to leave. We're at the gate in front of the house and the Buick is ready to go. My brother and I have been ready for hours, or so it seems. I tug at my Mother's hand, but she's elsewhere, awash in tears. I really can't think why. We're off on an aeroplane—what could be better. But Mom doesn't see this journey my way at all. She has already wept her way through the house and checked that all the furniture is covered with white sheets. Covering the furniture with sheets to protect them against Egypt's wicked sun usually means going to Alexandria for the summer. I've loved everything about those summers except for the endless naps we children have to sustain until we can go onto the beach again.
>
> But this trip isn't to Alexandria. There has been endless talk in the house of "America." And I know it's serious because whenever it comes up, Mom develops an errand for me to run. . . .

Every one of those seemingly small details is recognizably true. What child hasn't heard adults whispering of plans not meant for children to hear?

I asked the woman from Egypt if she had ever written anything like that before. She never had. Amazing! Why did it take almost 60 years? She was not a timid person; she told our class that she had recently bicycled from Berlin to Copenhagen. Why doesn't that confidence carry over to writing?

Dare to tell the smallest of stories if you want to generate large emotions.

Hold the Emotion!

DON'T SET OUT TO WRITE A HEART-TUGGING MEMOIR

TWENTY YEARS AGO I wrote an article in the *New York Times*, less than a thousand words long, that readers tell me they still remember for its high emotional content. But in writing it I had no such intention. Here's how the piece began:

> Every so often I find on my answering machine in mid-Manhattan a brief cry for help. "What should be done to stop water stains coming through the ceiling?" the voice asks, or "Is it O.K. to use primer-sealer 1-2-3 for peeling paint in the bathroom?" I don't know anything about water stains and peeling paint. I'm a writer. The callers are trying to reach William Zinsser & Co., my father's shellac business. The company was in New York so long—well over a century—that some old customers think it's still there, and when they call directory assistance the number they're given is mine. I'm the only William Zinsser still doing

business in New York; the firm moved away in 1975 and was later sold out of the family.

I don't mind getting the calls. Many of them are from hardware dealers in places like Moline and Winston-Salem and Fargo, and they remind me how much my father loved being an American businessman. But I also get calls from homeowners who are fixing up their home and want product information. I call them all back to give them the company's telephone number in New Jersey. That's how I learned about Barbara Wallenstein and the trouble she was having with her picket fence in Newtown, Connecticut.

That article was born of the desperation familiar to every freelance writer stuck for a subject. I came to my office one morning empty of ideas. "Please, God, just send me *something*," I thought. At such times of drought I'm grateful for the merest wisp of a topic, and that's what I got: the fact that in my life as a writer I hear from people who want to know how to spackle their bathroom. That's enough for one piece: a surprising oddity.

But as I started to write, other themes began tugging at my sleeve, and they all belonged in my story. How could I write about the phone messages and not talk about my father, and about his dream of the day I would join him in the business. It had been in the same family on the same block for well over a century, and I was his only son, the fourth William Zinsser. But my dream was to be a newspaperman, and I had to explain how my father accepted that disappointment and gave me his blessing, freeing me to succeed or fail on my own terms—the best gift a parent can bestow. And how one of my sisters' husbands was persuaded to come into the business. And how my father's values as a businessman and as an engaged citizen of New York would shape my own lifelong values as a journalist.

So the piece ended up being about many so-called universal themes: fathers and sons, family businesses, family expectations, filial duty, the continuity of cities, and several more. But I didn't set out to write about any of those themes; the story itself just gradually told me what it was about. If I had set out to write an emotional piece—"Boy, this is heart-tugging stuff!"—it would have tugged at no hearts.

Here's how the article ended:

> The integrity of my father's product came back to me one morning when I heard the beseeching voice of Mrs. Wallenstein on my answering machine. She was calling, she said, at 8:30 A.M. She had awakened with the resolve that this was the day her picket fence was finally going to get painted. She had a gallon of Zinsser's B-I-N and she needed to know if she could use it on the fence. Would I call back as soon as possible?
>
> I got to my office around 10—writers' hours start later than shellac scions' hours—and called Mrs. Wallenstein. She was right by the phone. "I realized as soon as I got up today," she said, "that my husband is never going to paint that fence." I told her that although I was the son who didn't go into the business, she was calling about the one product I happened to know as a user, and I was sorry to have to tell her that it should only be used indoors. She was no less sorry to hear it. I gave her the company's New Jersey phone number, explaining that it had been gone from 59th Street for more than 15 years.
>
> "I'm sure if you look at that can of B-I-N," I said, "the label gives the address as Somerset, New Jersey."

"I've got the can right here," she told me. "It says 516 West 59th Street."

"How long have you had that can, Mrs. Wallenstein?" I asked.

"Well, I guess we must have brought it with us when we moved from Long Island," she said.

We talked for a while about how "only yesterday" is always farther back than we think, and about how long it takes husbands to paint picket fences, and about fathers and sons and family businesses. Neither of us was in any hurry to get off the phone.

At the end Mrs. Wallenstein said, "It was very nice of you to call."

I said, "My father would have wanted me to."

Trapped by the Past

FINDING A DIFFERENT TAKE ON
JOHN HORNE BURNS'S STORY

OF ALL THE PIECES in this book, the hardest to write was "No Second Act" (page 19). It was about the forgotten American writer John Horne Burns, whose World War II novel *The Gallery*, published in 1947 to great acclaim, made him briefly famous. Reading it then, I could hardly believe how closely Burns's story paralleled my own coming of age as a young GI in North Africa and Italy. I still remember that gift with gratitude, and now I wanted to try to make sense of his short, disappointed life.

I had written about Burns once before, in 1990, when the Book-of-the-Month Club reissued *The Gallery* in a special edition and asked me to write a new introduction.

Eager to give the members their money's worth, I wrote a lengthy travel memoir and critical appraisal that I was quite pleased with. Now, for my blog, I thought I would just need to cut and reshape that earlier essay.

I found it in my files and began reading . . . and reading . . . and reading. The opening paragraph was followed by nine paragraphs—*nine paragraphs!*—describing my wonderment at being suddenly immersed in an Arab land unimaginably different from my Ivy League upbringing. Two entire paragraphs were devoted to the French architecture and Arab street life of Algiers.

As travel writing and as military history it was interesting stuff. Algiers in the spring of 1944 was a waiting room for the Allied invasion of southern France. "Probably," I wrote, "no other wartime city had such a mixed wardrobe of Allied uniforms walking its streets: Americans, Britons, Australians, New Zealanders, Canadians, Free French, Free Poles, Brazilians, Gurkhas, Senegalese, and 'Goums'—small, fierce-looking tribal warriors from France's military outposts in the Sahara."

But wasn't that piece supposed to be about John Horne Burns, not about me? My only connection to Burns was that he wrote a book that helped me to process my own war. Now I realized that I had become the captive of my own life narrative. I would have to start from scratch. As writers, we all do. There's no free lunch.

My first task was to squeeze all that preliminary material—my interest in Burns as a helpful figure in my life—into as few words as possible without squeezing it dry. That job took only a dozen sentences:

> In 1944 I was a 21-year-old army private, formerly a sheltered son of the Eastern Establishment, newly deposited in

Casablanca. I was in North Africa! *Me*! Nobody in my life had ever mentioned the Arabs. Our heritage was Europe; everything else was terra incognita.

The next day my fellow GIs and I were loaded onto a train of "forty-and-eights," decrepit wooden boxcars first used by the French army in World War I to carry 40 men or eight horses. Eight horses would have been more comfortable. For six days I sat in the open door of that boxcar with my legs hanging out over Morocco, Algeria, and Tunisia, a wide-eyed kid on a sensory high, intoxicated by new sights and sounds and smells. I loved the hubbub at the stations—Fez! Sidi Bel-Abbes! Oujda!—and I romanticized the Arabs themselves, even the skinny kids with beautiful smiles who ran alongside our train and pestered us for C rations and cigarettes.

Soon enough I would understand that the Arabs weren't "picturesque." They were a severely deprived people, many with skin and eye diseases that modern medicine knew how to cure. It was the beginning of, if not wisdom, at least the knowledge that "abroad" is a complicated place, not reducible to travel-poster simplicities.

That wrapped it up for me; the rest was about Burns. It was a complicated story, with flashbacks and flash-forwards and many psychological levels. It could only be told if readers were fed chunks of information *in the order they needed to understand the next chunk.*

First. What wartime Naples was like: a brutally bombed and degraded city. Its emotional heart—the organizing motif of Burns's book—was a huge arcade called the Galleria Umberto, a 24-hour hub of black-market buying and selling.

Next. Burns's place in the literature of World War II. The early blockbuster books, like *The Naked and the Dead*, were novels of combat that didn't speak to my experience. *The Gallery* did.

Next. Who Burns was: his earlier life as a private-school English teacher.

Next. The structure of *The Gallery* and its central theme: Burns's gradual loss of innocence. How he came to hate the privileged arrogance of American soldiers and to love the destitute Italians, thereby anticipating by a generation the hubris of Vietnam and the idea of "the ugly American."

Next. Burns's postwar life: his bitterness over the critics' savage reviews of his second novel and his decline into drink and early death.

Next. How *The Gallery* holds up today. How, rereading it, I saw—as I couldn't have known in 1947—that it foreshadowed such World War II classics as *The Caine Mutiny. Mister Roberts, Catch-22,* and *Naples '44.*

My essay, in short, was a composition exercise. I didn't enjoy writing it, but I loved having written it. It's airtight, I think, and it says in 1,000 words everything that really needs to be known about Burns and his legacy. It taught me to beware of the past as a launching pad for writing about the present. The past is often a trap.

Memory, Memoir, and Loss

WHAT I LEARNED FROM A 9/11 FIREFIGHTER

As A BOY I never kept watch for the first robin. My eye was out for the first newspaper articles from the small Florida towns where the major league baseball teams went for spring training. Bradenton! Lakeland! Clearwater! Vero Beach! "Come on down!" those places called to me, and I vowed that some day I would.

That day came in March 1982 when I was driving through central Florida and saw a sign to Winter Haven, the spring training camp of the Boston Red Sox. My rented car, like a good horse, knew the way, and soon I was settled in the grandstand with a hot dog and a beer. The sun was warm, the grass was green, and the air was alive with the sounds of rebirth: bat meeting ball, ball meeting glove, players and coaches chattering across the diamond. Winter Haven indeed! Winter Heaven was more like it.

I was sitting in a sea of codgers, codging the time away. A rookie left-hander was on the mound, warming up for an intra-squad game. I was enjoying his form, wondering if this was his year to make it to the majors. I told the man next to me that the kid reminded me of Warren Spahn. The man said he looked like Preacher Roe. His wife said he was a ringer for Harvey Haddix. An old codger mentioned Lefty Grove. A young codger mentioned Vida Blue. We were typical springtime fools, seeing what we wanted to see.

Many years later, recalling that moment in my book *Spring Training*, I wrote:

> So the afternoon slipped by in contentment. The ancient rhythms of baseball were intact; we could have been watching a game in 1882, not 1982. No organist toyed with our emotions, no electronic scoreboard told us when to cheer. We were suspended in a pocket of time unlike any other moment in baseball's long year. It was a time of renewal for the players and also for the fans. It was a time for looking both forward and back: forward to the new season

and as far back as the oldest codger could recall. And what made it all work was memory. Memory was the glue that held baseball together as the continuing American epic.

A few years ago I used that passage in my memoir-writing class to suggest how to write about a place. Mere facts, I said, aren't sufficient ("our house was on Spruce Street," "the neighbors had a dog named Spot"). The task is to find the *point* of the place—its identifying idea. It may be waiting for you to find it. Or you may have to impose on the place some larger idea of your own. In the case of my afternoon in Winter Haven, the point of the place is memory. That's what the passage is "about."

One student, Thomas Ryan, was a firefighter who had been on duty in the World Trade Center on 9/11. "I don't think the piece is about memory," he said. "I think it's about loss."

That hit me like a boxer's punch. I was so sure my piece was about memory, so pleased with my tidy organizing idea. But then I thought: Tom Ryan is the expert here, not me. A firefighter who was in one of those collapsing towers knows everything there is to know about loss. Tom made me realize that I also was in the loss business.

I thought of all the stories that have been told in my class for 20 years. Some of the tellers are old Jewish men and women who survived the Nazi camps and are still haunted by the death and dispersal of their families. Some are men and women trying to recapture the lost landscape of their childhood—the much-loved small-town Main Street that's now mostly strip malls. Some are middle-aged women whose lives are still stalled on the day their father died when they were children.

Baseball would seem to be a safe writer's subject. Yet the classics of baseball literature—Ring Lardner's *You Know Me Al*, Mark Harris's *Bang the Drum Slowly*, Roger Kahn's *The Boys of Summer*—are tinged with sadness. The reality of baseball is no different from anyone else's reality. Even the boys of summer grow old.

Writing for the Wrong Reasons

PUBLISHERS DON'T NECESSARILY
HAVE THE ANSWERS

DEPRESSINGLY OFTEN I hear from people who are stalled on a piece of writing for reasons that have nothing to do with actual writing. They are snarled in the machinery of trying to market what they write. Here are three typical recent examples.

A woman I'll call Ravi, now in her 30s, came to see me from Ohio in a state of paralyzing indecision. She had grown up in India and had been a journalist there. Now, settled in America with her husband and two children, she met and came to admire an older woman, Mrs. X, who founded various humanitarian projects abroad. Ravi wrote and sold articles about three of those projects, and it occurred to her, as it does to all freelancers who have invested time in a subject, to write more pieces about Mrs. X and publish them all as a book.

But as she proceeded she began to feel a strong tug to write about her girlhood in India and thereby try to understand the despotic father who derided her own ambitions. Her agent told her to stick with Mrs. X, but after a few months she found herself immobilized. That's when she came to see me.

When Ravi described Mrs. X's projects she sounded like a journalist. But when she began talking about her complicated girlhood she sounded like a daughter. Hearing that shift in the emotional weight of her voice, I told her that India was her true subject. The book about Mrs. X was somebody else's story; any competent journalist could write it.

Then she spoke the killer sentence: "My agent says that if I publish my book about Mrs. X, it will give me the credential I need to find a publisher for my book about India."

That's not a good reason for writing a book. It's a marketing reason, not a writer's reason. It's also not necessarily true. Ravi's book would take two years of her life to research and complete, and even then it might not have enough variety; the chapters could begin to sound alike. But agents can't afford such thoughts; their eye is on the contract, not on the writer. Of course Ravi's India memoir also might not get published, but she would be fully alive while writing it. She would grow as a writer and as a person.

The other day—example number two—I ran into a friend I'll call Melanie. A respected horticulturist, she has published three successful books and she also lectures widely; she's not a supplicant begging for crumbs at the temple door. When I asked what she was working on, she said, "I'm writing one book for love and one book for money." Another terrible sentence. She said she could only afford to write the book she has always wanted to write—a nontraditional book about edible plants—if she first wrote the big-money book on how to grow orchids at home.

"But there's no joy in it," she told me. "The publisher laid out the template in advance, and they're always after me to add more words than I need to explain what the reader requires. They'll call and say, 'You only sent us 200 words and we need 600 to 800, so please send us at least another page.'" Melanie is a fierce enemy of avoidable sludge; her style is simple and strong. Now, lashed to her computer like a galley slave, she says, "I keep coming up with longer ways to say something—little clauses that don't really mean anything." That's also not a good reason for writing a book. It's a designer's reason, nothing less than writer abuse. And reader abuse.

Of course I know that writers, like everyone else, have to pay the bills. But I believe that blind subservience to an imagined final product is harmful to body and soul and is also often unnecessary. A few weeks ago—example number three—a young writer from California came to see me. He, too, isn't a novice; he has been a magazine editor, and he writes a likable column in a local paper. He arrived in a state of high anxiety over an interview the next day and wanted advice on how to prepare for it.

Who was this mighty personage he was about to confront? It was an agent. He hoped to persuade the agent to take him on as a client. Would he be found worthy? To him it was obviously a boss-and-servant relationship. He was amazed when I told him that the agent was *his* servant and *he* was the person in charge. He was the creator of the product that the agent needed to pay his own bills. I gave the writer permission to believe in himself, and he left looking like what he was—a bright and confident young man ready to move the world.

Please! Try not to acquiesce too quickly in projects that you know aren't right for who you are. Think about other financial solutions that will free you to focus on the primary task of becoming a writer. Give more thought to the longer trajectory of your life. Your most important work-in-progress is not the story you're working on now. Your most important work-in-progress is you.

Rescued by Humor

MORE THOUGHTS ON LESS SERIOUSNESS

HUMOR IS NOT a sweetener to be added when a sad story needs a few laughs. It's a special angle of vision, given to some people and not to others, integral to their personality, and for memoir writers it's a lifesaver.

In the second sentence of his best-selling memoir *Angela's Ashes*, Frank McCourt wonders how he survived his boyhood in the slums of Limerick. I think I know: he was saved by humor. I've never heard of a childhood more squalid than McCourt's, yet his book is repeatedly funny. A special angle of vision enabled him to see beyond the poverty to the black comedy of a social structure gone so disastrously wrong, and when he wrote his memoir, half a century later, that vision was still intact, enabling him to recall his early years with love and forgiveness. Without humor he couldn't have survived his childhood, and without humor he couldn't have written his book.

One of my favorite memoirs is V. S. Pritchett's *A Cab at the Door*, which takes its title from the carriage that always seemed to be waiting outside to whisk the family to new lodgings, just ahead of his father's creditors. Sent away from home in his teens and apprenticed to the London leather trade, Pritchett had a 19th-century boyhood, Dickensian in its hardship. Yet he recalls those years with a certain merriment and even with gratitude. No whining.

Whining crept into the American memoir in the mid-1990s. Until then the world of letters adhered to an agreed-upon code of civility, drawing a veil over emotions and events too private or shameful to reveal. Then talk shows were born and shame went out to the window. Memoirists sprouted from the American soil like dandelions. Using memoir as therapy, they bashed their parents and brothers and sisters and relatives and teachers and coaches and everyone else who ever misunderstood them—a new class of self-appointed victims. Today nobody remembers those books; readers won't put up with whining. But V. S. Pritchett survived his boyhood to become one of the master writers of the 20th century, his stories and essays a reservoir of wisdom and compassion.

For me, an enlisted man in World War II, Joseph Heller's *Catch-22* is the book that most closely captures the everyday lunacy of military life, just as Stanley Kubrick's *Dr. Strangelove* is the movie that most closely captures the insanity of the nuclear arms race. Like Heller's Captain Yossarian, maniacally trapped by official decisions that began in logic and imperceptibly crossed over into the absurd, I often asked myself, as has every soldier going back to Hadrian's legions building a wall across northern England, "How did I end up doing *this*?"

One day, at my army base in Algeria, our unit commander, Colonel Monro McCloskey, never a stickler for the separation of military and personal business, ordered some of us GIs to build him a rock garden outside his tent. How funny is that.

~~~~~~~~~~~~~~~~~~~~~~~~~~~~~~~~—

A Joyful Noise

LIGHTEN UP, EVEN WHEN YOUR STORY IS DARK

A FEW SUMMERS ago I heard that the historian David McCullough would be giving the commencement address at a fine-arts college in a small Connecticut town, and, finding myself in the area, I went around to listen. McCullough is my role model for his honorable conduct as a writer, and on this occasion, as always, his values were solid.

The graduating class only had 25 young men and women, and it would have been easy for McCullough to give a standard commencement talk, exhorting the young to go forth with high hopes and high ideals and love of country. Of course he didn't. The code of honor says: Do it right. There's no free lunch. He had written a talk specifically for those newborn artists—a talk generously furnished with helpful admonitions by great artists of the past. The one that I wrote down was by the American painter Robert Henri: "You should paint like a man coming over the top of the hill singing."

Amen. That's also how you should write, sing, dance, draw, sculpt, act, play an instrument, take a photograph, design a building, live a life. I often think I'm the only teacher who talks about enjoyment as a crucial ingredient in writing. My students seem puzzled that I keep coming back to the subject, that I find so much amusement in what I see and hear and read every day. Life is serious! Writing is serious! Most writers take the act of writing with grim solemnity, fearful that they won't be worthy of the gods of literature scowling down from Mount Parnassus. Or is it that they take *themselves* so seriously?

When I write I make a conscious effort to generate a sense of enjoyment— to convey to my readers that I found the events I'm describing more than ordinarily interesting, or unusual, or amusing, or emotional, or bizarre. Otherwise why bother to describe them? I also try to convey the idea that I was feeling great when I did my writing— which I almost never was; writing well is hard work. But readers have a right to believe that you were having a good time taking them on your chosen voyage.

So, please, lighten up, even when the story you're telling is a dark one. The family that you remember as impossibly dysfunctional also had a lot funny stuff going on. Humor will get you out of some of life's most painful corners, as Frank McCourt proved in *Angela's Ashes*.

The Right to Write

GETTING PUBLISHED ISN'T THE ONLY
REASON TO WRITE YOUR STORY

BECAUSE I'VE LONG TAUGHT a course in memoir writing and have frequently written about that form, I often hear from people who want to be sure I didn't miss still another article expressing horror that so many bad memoirs keep being published. The latest object of their wrath is a recent essay in the *New York Times Book Review* by Neil Genzlinger, a staff editor.

His piece doesn't say anything new; the same article has been repeatedly written since the memoir craze erupted 15 years ago. That was one thing that annoyed my callers. But what angered them was the writer's pious tone. Genzlinger's essay is sky-high on the smugness meter. He says, "Sorry to be so harsh" (which I doubt), "but this flood just has to be stopped. We don't have that many trees left." Literary criticism meets forestry.

In his review Genzlinger trashes three new memoirs, which, for him, typify a body of work by "people you've never heard of, writing uninterestingly about the unexceptional, apparently not realizing how commonplace their little wrinkle is or how many other people have already written about it. . . . That's what happens when immature people write memoirs. . . . Nobody wants to relive your misery." His message is: Don't even think of writing your stupid memoir.

Sorry to be so harsh, but I don't like people telling other people they shouldn't write about their life. All of us earn that right by being born; one of the deepest human impulses is to leave a record of what we did and what we thought and felt on our journey. The issue here is not whether so many bad memoirs should be written. It's whether they should be *published*—let's put the blame where it belongs—and whether, once published, they should be reviewed. The *Times* can use its space more helpfully than by allowing a critic to hyperventilate on an exhausted subject. We don't have that many trees left.

Memoirs first got a bad name in the mid-1990s. Until that time authors adhered to an agreed-upon code of modesty, drawing a veil over their most shameful acts and feelings. Then talk shows were born and shame went out the window. Overnight, no recollected event was too squalid, no family too dysfunctional, to be trotted out, for the titillation of the masses, on television and in magazines and books. Memoir became the new therapy. Everybody and his brother wallowed in their struggle with alcohol, drug addiction, recovery, abuse, illness, aging parents, troubled children, codependency, and other newly fashionable syndromes, meanwhile bashing their parents, siblings, teachers, coaches, and everyone else who ever dared to misunderstand them. It was a new literature of victimhood.

But nobody remembered those books for more than 10 minutes; readers won't put up with whining. The memoirs that endure from that period are the ones that look back with love and forgiveness. Writers like Frank McCourt (*Angela's Ashes*), Mary Karr (*The Liars' Club*), Tobias Wolff (*This Boy's Life*), Pete Hamill (*A Drinking Life*), and Russell Baker (*Growing Up*) are as hard on their young selves as they are on their elders, elevating the pain of the past by arriving at a larger truth about the brokenness of families. We are not victims, they want us to know. We come from a tribe of fallible people, and we have survived to tell the story and get on with our lives.

There are many good reasons for writing your memoir that have nothing to do with being published. One is to leave your children and grandchildren a record of who you were and what heritage they were born into. Please get started on that; time tends to surprise us by running out. One of the saddest sentences I know is "I wish I had asked my mother about that."

Another reason is to paint a portrait of the town or community, now considerably changed, where you grew up. Somewhere on the shelves of every American small-town library and historical society is a makeshift volume, often written by a retired schoolteacher, that resuscitates a bygone way of life. This is a priceless gift to social historians—crucial information that isn't available anywhere else.

Writing is also a potent search mechanism, often as helpful as psychoanalysis and a lot cheaper. When you start on your memoir you'll find your subconscious mind delivering your past to you, recalling people and events you have entirely forgotten. That voyage of rediscovery is a pleasure in itself.

Finally, writing is a sanity-saving companion for people in times of grief, loss, illness, and other accidents of fate. Just getting down on paper those grim details—still another bout of surgery, still another befogged moment with a husband or wife lost to Alzheimer's—will validate your ordeal and make you feel less alone.

Most of those memoirs shouldn't be published. They are too raw and ragged, too self-absorbed and poorly written, seldom telling us anything we don't already know. But that doesn't mean you shouldn't write them. Don't worry about the trees.

3

Tech Age

Nowhere People

LOOK IN THE glove compartment of my car and you won't see a single glove. But you will find maps—tattered maps of places I once visited. I can look at road maps of the United States forever, reminding myself of strangers met along the way, of small roads with small towns of unexpected beauty, of farms and fairgrounds and Civil War battlefields, of college towns where I once taught, of the never-far-from-my-thoughts Mississippi River, the majestic highway that bisects the nation. I like to situate myself in the larger universe of continents and rivers and oceans that I was born into.

But with the advent of global positioning I've begun to wonder if I belong to a vanishing tribe. Today's drivers don't seem to care where they actually are; they only want to know where they are going. Cradled by the soothing voice of Kathy or Sandra telling them to turn right at the next intersection and left after the bank, they are absolved from looking at the contours of the land, the horses in the field, the buildings and stores along Main Street that give every town its identity.

The other day I happened to notice that the huge map of the New York City subway system, a comforting friend affixed to the wall of every subway station, has been supplemented by a small linear strip that only shows the successive stops along that particular subway line. Gone, for many riders, is the knowledge that they are traveling on one of the world's great railway networks—227 miles of tracks that run over two big bridges and under two rivers, connecting four of the city's five boroughs at their remotest extreme, from Woodlawn cemetery in the Bronx to the ocean-side cottages in Far Rockaway, often emerging from a tunnel to an elevated stretch that offers a breathtaking view of the towers of Manhattan. Such a city is not reducible to one short, straight line.

When our son John was a small boy I used to take him on elevated subway rides to no particular destination. We would stand in the front car, enjoying the interlaced switches ahead of us and the ethnic neighborhoods below; at one stop four Ecuadorian musicians got on and filled the car with song. Our pleasure was in the journey, not the arrival, because we never had a place to arrive.

A generation later I was once left in charge of my grandson Mark, who was then about 10. He expected me to take him, as instructed by his mother, to the Central Park Zoo and F. A. O. Schwarz. Instead we took the Lexington Avenue subway to the City Hall stop. "The city looks different down here," Mark said when we emerged, referring to the smaller scale of the buildings and the helter-skelter pattern of the streets. I explained that this was the oldest part of the city. We walked across the Brooklyn Bridge, stopping to look down on the narrowing tip of Manhattan and the once-busy docks with names like Peck Slip. We saw—as if on a map—how the East River joins the Hudson River near the Statue of Liberty and flows down a channel to the Atlantic Ocean and the whole wide world. On the walkway of the bridge we actually *touched* its mighty cables where they were anchored in a giant concrete slab. Our old and young fingers made contact with one of the wonders of 19th-century industrial America. Afterward we walked through Chinatown, just north of the bridge. Mark had no idea that such an exotic community existed just a short subway ride from the tidy uptown neighborhoods he was familiar with.

On our expedition Mark and I were fully alive in our surroundings. Not so today's urban walkers. The new hand-held technologies have sired a breed of elsewhere-dwellers, incurious about the here and now, texting or chatting on a cell phone to someone in Dubai. They have no idea where Dubai is. They could look at a map. But they won't.

No Place Like "Home"

HISTORIAN V. NEW YORK TIMES HINGES ON THE MEANING OF "HOME DELIVERY"

MY WIFE IS LOCKED in semantic combat with the *New York Times.* As a historian she has long made extensive use of the free online *Times* archives for her research, grateful for its boundless access to historical information. Recently the *Times* began to charge a fee for that access. Fair enough; the newspaper is entitled to get paid for such a heroic act of retrieval. That's not the issue.

The issue is that the *Times* will waive the fee for customers who already subscribe to the paper by home delivery. But what is "home delivery?" That depends on the age of the *Times* salesperson on the phone trying to explain the new system.

In our household "home delivery" means that a physical object—a newspaper—is brought to the subscriber's "home" every morning. The home itself is also a physical object—a house, an apartment, a trailer, or some other edifice where families are raised, meals are cooked, and memories are kept. Wherever our family has perched, the *Times* has been there to greet us every morning, lying on the doormat, faithful as an old dog.

When the *Times* salesperson, presumably a child of the digital generation, asked my wife for proof that we receive "home delivery" she gave him the name of our independent delivery company. He didn't know what service that might be. He wouldn't accept the name and insisted on proper proof of home delivery. What better proof, my wife wondered, than the corporate name of the elves who drive trucks through the sleeping city with their sacred bales of newsprint?

Finally it dawned on her that the *Times* person selling "home delivery" was not picturing an actual home. "Home" was the home page of the *Times* on a computer screen. He had evidently never thought of his employer's product as a physical object, never heard of "newsboys," kids enshrined in American folklore for their ability to toss a newspaper from a moving bicycle so that it skidded to a perfect stop on the customer's front porch. That boy in a visored cap was long a standard figure in comic strips and Hollywood movies; many titans of the American dream began their rags-to-riches ascent as newsboys.

Was that teenage labor force now unremembered? It came back to me that when my grandson spent a summer with me in New York a few years ago he never looked at the *New York Times* that I brought in every morning from outside our apartment door, where it had been home delivered. He got the day's news from a computer that was already somewhere inside the house.

No winner has yet emerged in the case of *Historian v. New York Times*. Neither side understands what the other is talking about. Seeking further clarification, my wife consulted the *Times* web page and found that the paper has added three more "home delivery" options: the *NYTimes.com* smartphone app, the *NYTimes.com* tablet app, and the *NYTimes.com* all-digital access app.

The Historian was not pleased to learn of these additional routes to her grail of research; they didn't sound much like "home delivery." Such is the linguistic crevasse that separates the generations. In another decade, "home" will no longer be the place where Robert Frost says they have to take you in. Home will be any place that has a computer.

Me and My Relationships

SANDRA IS GIVING ME UP FOR BRAD

LAST WEEK I got a letter from the man I once thought of as my broker, who now calls himself my investment counselor and would probably call himself my wealth management adviser if I had any "wealth" for him to manage. He was writing to tell me that Sandra, "the lead assistant assigned to your relationship, has decided to change careers and become a full-time mother of 10-month-old Brad."

I didn't even know I *had* a relationship with Sandra. She never mentioned it, probably because she already had

a relationship—evidently quite a long one—with the father of 10-month-old Brad. But my investment counselor
said he was "happy to announce" that Daniele had joined
his office and would now be managing my relationship.

A few days later I went into my Citibank branch to get
some cash and found a message on the ATM. It said, "Now
you can have a dedicated relationship manager!" That got
me wondering about Daniele. I knew she would be caring.
But shouldn't she also be *dedicated*?

I decided to review my other relationships. Franco, my
barber, is sensitive to my every whim. He knows exactly
where I don't want him to use clippers, and he never lets
those little hairs slip down between my neck and my col-
lar. Maria, at the coffee shop, is exquisitely attuned to our
relationship. She knows when it's so cold outside that I
would want soup. Jerry, my laundryman, never forgets to
say "Have a nice day" when I drop off my shirts.

Somehow it never occurred to me that I was having a relationship with those men and women. I thought
they were just old-fashioned merchants. Obviously what
they need is an important job title. If they worked in the
financial or the business sector they could be relationship managers. Better yet they could be associates. Half
the employees in corporate America are associates. When
I'm kept waiting on the telephone, a robot voice says, "All
our associates are currently assisting other customers."
(Everyone who keeps us waiting is doing something "currently.") At my post office an automated voice tells me to
"proceed to the associate at window 14." When I reach
window 14 that person doesn't look like an associate. He
or she looks like a postal clerk. That's an honorable job

honorably performed by the United States Postal Service at least since the 19th century.

My problem with "relationship" is that it means whatever anyone needs it to mean. It doesn't denote a specific act—like, say, "falling in love" or "getting married." Those bold leaps of faith have long been sung by poets and troubadours. But nowhere in bardic lore is there any word of Antony's relationship with Cleopatra, or Tristan's relationship with Isolde, or Romeo's relationship with the girl on the balcony. Cole Porter didn't write "let's do it, let's have a relationship." He wrote "let's fall in love." That's what people used to do.

I became a student of modern relationships by reading the wedding announcements in the *New York Times*. Not so long ago those articles only reported the facts: the bride wore a gown of *peau de soie*, the groom was descended from someone listed in the *Domesday Book*. But lately they have swollen to include little narratives in which the bride and groom recall their long and labyrinthine journey to the altar. Not unlike *Pride and Prejudice* in their repeated failures of nerve, those accounts go something like this:

Binky still remembers the day in 1997 when she first met Josh. "I was scuba diving in Antigua," she says, "and I saw this cute guy with big pecs and curly hair and I knew he was the man of my dreams. We agreed to meet again, and in 1999 I was skiing in Gstaad and I saw this cute guy with a lot of snow in his curly hair, and I'm like, 'Omigod! Isn't that Josh?'"

"It was like lightning struck," Josh recalls, "and I told myself 'I've got to see more of that girl!'" In 2000 he invited Binky to a wine tasting at the Yale Club. They hit it off over "a really neat Chardonnay," and a few weeks later they began

dating and in 2002 they moved in together. "Last year we were at a film festival in Marrakech," Binky remembers, "and there was a big orange moon over the Atlas Mountains, and Josh looked at me in this funny way and he said, 'You know, maybe we should think about getting married.'"

Central Park Lite

EXPERIENTIAL OPTIMIZATION
IN THE APP BRIGADE

CENTRAL PARK AND I go back almost as far as a man and a park can go. In the early 1930s, when my sisters and I were children, we sometimes stayed overnight with our grandmother, who lived at 1 West 69th Street. Unskilled at amusing the young, she would give us loaves of stale bread, saved for just such an emergency, and send us across the street into the park to feed the sheep.

At that time Central Park had a flock of 300 sheep that grazed on the vast Sheep Meadow, as it's still called today, and thereby kept it mowed. They were housed in an edifice that was built especially for them in 1871, just inside the park at 67th Street. Ambitious beyond the usual dreams of sheepfold architecture, it had Victorian Gothic gables and spires and was clothed in polychrome red brick—a masonry style that would become the signature of all the park's small buildings. This was the temple to which my sisters and I came bearing our gift of stale bread. Seeing us, the sheep would poke their snouts through slots in the fence that enclosed their courtyard and would nibble at our childish fingers.

In 1934 the sheep were dispossessed, the Central Park shepherd was retired, and the building was leased to a businessman who converted it into a restaurant called The Tavern on the Green, where a different kind of sheep came to be fed. He decorated the interior in High Bordello style, with glittering mirrors and crystal chandeliers, and in that guise it became a favored roost for tourists and wedding parties. Two years ago it reverted to the Parks Department, which has since stripped away the Tavern's glitz and is looking for a new tenant.

But even without my sheep it's still my Central Park, never far from my thoughts—a landscape of amazing trees and interlaced paths and lakes and bridges set apart from the city's rectilinear grid. My wife goes there to look for birds. The bird I go looking for is a jazz saxophonist who once played with Earl Hines's band and now freelances on the Great Mall. I sit on a park bench with a hot dog and a lot of mustard and bask in the melodies of Harold Arlen and Duke Ellington.

Around me, people of every age and size move to every known mode of locomotion. They walk, they jog, they run, they bike, they skateboard, they roller-skate, they Rollerblade, they get pushed in strollers, they break dance, they hip-hop, often to Afro-Cuban rhythms slapped on drums. Just north of where I sit, couples in rowboats circumnavigate a lake that looks just as it did when it was drawn for Currier & Ives. Farther north, baseball teams compete on diamonds with real backstops. Elsewhere, people play chess, tennis, croquet, and bowls. In the winter they ice-skate and go sledding. Farther north, in Harlem Meer, they fish. It's a park where people have always been able to figure out what they want to do and where to do it.

I was therefore startled, the other day, to see an advertisement by the Central Park Conservancy, the nonprofit agency that rescued the park from decay and despair 20 years ago and has since nurtured it with utmost care and love. "Download our app," the ad said, "and experience Central Park right in the palm of your hand." I understand the purpose of the ad: to make the park's resources more widely known to potential visitors and supporters.

But I also wondered if I was getting a glimpse of the future—of the day when every organization has an app and nobody goes anywhere. I already have an app for major league baseball. It's called a television set. I sit in my apartment and watch the Mets and the Yankees without paying the owners their piratical price for admission and food. Will the Metropolitan Museum of Art be next to join the app brigade? "Avoid the crowds! Download Rembrandt on your smartphone." Or the Museum of Natural History? "Simply click on dinosaur or whale."

With the approach of summer I'm hoping to hear of a new app created by Jones Beach, telling me what it feels like to romp in the surf and lie on the sand. "No more messy sunscreens! Now you can experience a day at the beach in the palm of your hand!"

Working for Tina Brown

IT'S ABOUT HOW TO COMMUNICATE

I STUDIED THE photograph on the front page of the *New York Times*—two standing figures—as if I were puzzling out an ancient glyph. What kind of society practiced such an odd tribal rite? The caption said: "Tina Brown with Stephen Colvin, chief of the Newsweek-Daily Beast Company." Ms. Brown, the high-buzz former editor of *Vanity Fair* and the *New Yorker* and of the defunct *Talk*, had once again reincarnated herself—as editor of *Newsweek*, a hybrid formed by merging the dying 78-year-old newsmagazine with her own dying website, the *Daily Beast*.

The first issue was due out momentarily, and in her *Times* interview—during which, "between answering questions, she clicked through her BlackBerry scanning e-mail"—Ms. Brown described the recent whirlwind of prenatal staff discussions. "It is not uncommon," the *Times* said, "for her senior editors to find themselves barraged with e-mails predawn or on weekends."

What puzzled me about the *Times*' caption was the preposition "with," suggesting that Ms. Brown and Mr. Colvin were chatting about their imminent baby. But in fact, though the two moguls were "with" each other, standing barely apart, both of them were sending text messages, thumbs fully engaged. They were "with" someone who was somewhere else.

Looking at the two texters, I wondered: Why aren't these people talking to each other? I also wondered if they were enjoying their work. That used to be a big reason why people became journalists: to give themselves—and their readers—a good time. That bug bit me when I was a young boy reading the *New York Herald Tribune*, which I would spread out on the rug because I was too small to hold it open. I marveled that a paper existed that seemed to have been written just for me. Its articles usually had an extra touch of humanity or humor—some gift of themselves that the reporters were offering to the world—and

I knew that that's what I wanted to do. I'm still trying to do it.

Home from World War II, I landed a job with the *Herald Tribune* and found myself in the same room—the vast and grimy city room—with the giants who first put that boyhood dream in my head. They were a mixed bag of mavericks and oddballs, unsurprised by human oddity. Nobody gave it a second thought when Lucius Beebe, the legendary fop, who covered "café society," arrived for work in midmorning wearing a derby, a bespoke suit, a magenta shirt, a white silk tie, and a figured vest with a gold watch and chain, or when the absent-minded music editor Francis D. Perkins, who often smoked his pipe upside down, started another paper fire in his wastebasket. We were a community held together by the common purpose of our daily voyage.

We spent far more time at the water cooler than our kidneys required, endlessly talking shop. None of us ever received a message from the executive editor predawn. George Cornish was a broad and cultivated man, and I can safely bet that at "predawn" he was fast asleep and that he later had a leisurely breakfast, reading the day's news and thinking about the world that his paper would have to navigate when he got to the office.

Many years later, when I wrote a column for *Life*, I learned that if certain editors had to be consulted it was wise to do so before their three-martini lunch. But the magazine always came out, and it conveyed a sense of high enjoyment. It was the glue that held America together before television came along.

I won't try to guess what nostrums of modern psycho-pharmacology lurk in the handbags and desk drawers of modern journalists. It wouldn't be easy to work for bosses who are chained to every last email, text message, and tweet. Such bosses leave their writers and editors no breathing room. Didn't anyone tell them that oxygen is the spark of life?

Stopping Steve Martin

WHEN GIVING THE PUBLIC
WHAT IT WANTS IS A BAD IDEA

PLEASE IMAGINE THAT it is May 29, 1913, and you are attending the world premiere of Igor Stravinsky's *The Rite of Spring*, choreographed by Nijinsky, at the Théâtre des Champs-Élysées in Paris. The conductor is Pierre Monteux. In its glitter and glamour and lofty expectations it is an event of highest wattage.

The music has barely begun when the audience, its ears long tuned to the orthodoxies of late-19th-century Romanticism, starts to register its hatred of Stravinsky's dissonant harmonies. Murmurs are heard. Then hisses and boos, which soon escalate into howls and shouts of protest. Stravinsky defenders argue boisterously with Stravinsky detractors, and some of them come to blows. Brawls erupt in various parts of the hall, and the police are called. But the rioting goes on.

Now please imagine that a representative of the management walks down the aisle to the conductor's podium and tugs at the coattails of Pierre Monteux. "Maestro, *je regrette*," he says, "the audience is not pleased with Monsieur Stravinsky's music. They say it hurts their ears. We wish you to play something they will like better."

Monteux stops the music and calls for an assistant to bring him a folder of other scores in the orchestra's repertoire. He selects a suite of Magyar peasant songs, which the musicians proceed to play. The audience returns to its seats and calm is restored to the Théâtre des Champs-Élysées.

Except for its denouement, that account of the premiere of *The Rite of Spring* is true. A century later it still ranks as the most tumultuous event in the history of classical performance. But in fact Monteux didn't lay down his baton. The orchestra played every note of Stravinsky's score, though much of what it played wasn't heard above the uproar. The band played on.

The band played on because the band always plays on. The actors always keep acting, the dancers keep dancing, the circus aerialists keep swinging from a trapeze. They finish the job they were hired to do, however boring or enigmatic it may be. The audience doesn't get to stop the show. That's the ancient contract between performer and ticket buyer. I doubt if anyone in a Greek amphitheater wandered down onto the stage to tell the actors playing Oedipus that the folks upstairs wanted something a little less knotty. The show may be hated, hooted at, slept through, walked out on. But stopped? Never!

Never? Two weeks ago in New York a show got stopped. At the 92nd Street Y, one of the city's most admired cultural citadels, Steve Martin, as advertised, was discussing art, the subject of his latest book, when the management handed a note to him and his co-host, the respected journalist Deborah Solomon. The note told them to stop talking about art and instead talk about Martin's movie and television career. It turned out that the Y, without telling Martin and Solomon, was also sending the program via closed-circuit television to an outside audience, and those viewers were peppering the Y with emails demanding more palatable fare. The two performers were shaken by the interruption, but they complied and gave the emailers the celebrity pap they wanted.

Reading about the event, I felt betrayed. I was further annoyed when the Y offered to give all the ticket buyers their money back, as if it had committed some shameful act. What's to be ashamed of? Steve Martin is one of our most serious and versatile artists—not only a comedian but an actor, writer, playwright, musician, composer, art connoisseur, and art collector.

In his remarks to the press afterward and in a later op-ed piece, Martin was generous and sweetly reasonable. Not me. I hated seeing him surrender to the *illiterati* in Twitterville. If that technology had existed in earlier decades we might never have seen *Waiting for Godot* or the plays of Ionesco or Harold Pinter.

I've spent hundreds of hours in the Y's auditorium listening to concerts and forums, most of them richly rewarding. If some of them were boring I held my tongue; that's the contract.

For Steve Martin's future use, I offer this response to his critics: Listen up, lunkheads! I came to talk about art. You got a problem with that? Get over it. —Steve

"Bring Back Boredom!"
REWIRE MULTITASK TENDENCIES

I HAVE A lot of pen pals and phone pals, most of whom I've never met. Sometimes one of them makes it to New York and I get to connect the voice on the phone or the person on the page with its matching face and shape. Usually there's no resemblance to my long-imagined friend.

Last week I was visited by a writer from the Midwest, in town with her husband "to see some shows." Over the years she had occasionally called me to talk over some point of writing or teaching, and I was looking forward to getting to know her better. She duly arrived at my office in mid-Manhattan and we settled down to catch up. Although she now lives in another state, she explained, she was born in New York City, at a long-gone institution called the New York Lying-in Hospital. "As a matter of fact," she said, "I think it was right around here, on one of these blocks."

I asked her to tell me about her life and her work, but suddenly I realized that she was no longer looking at me. She was fussing with her iPod, grimacing into its tiny screen. I thought maybe she had received a message about a sick child or a husband lost in the New York subway system.

Finally I said, "What are you doing with that thing?"

She said, "I'm trying to find out where the Lying-in Hospital used to be."

My face, which she had resumed looking at, must have suggested that I didn't care where the Lying-in Hospital used to be.

"What's the matter?" she said. "Don't you want me to multitask?"

"*No!*" I said. I was practically screaming at her. "I want you to *mono*-task!" She looked as if she didn't know if she could do that.

I know I'm not reporting a new social phenomenon; the rudeness of multitaskers is now so habitual that it's no longer even perceived as rude. But for me that writer's visit was a tipping point. For the first time I understood the heroin-like tug of constantly available information. The address of the Lying-in Hospital was in no way pertinent to what the writer had come to talk about; she could have looked it up later. But she was hooked. I saw that if data exists, it has to be accessed, whatever the cost in friendship or civility. Information trumps conversation.

That trend was massively confirmed a few days later in a *New York Times* article called "Growing Up Digital, Wired for Distraction," which explored the growing difficulty for teachers trying to reach students who are less and less able to sustain attention. "Their brains are rewarded not for staying on task but for jumping to the next thing," said Michael Rich, a professor at Harvard Medical School and executive director of the Center on Media and Child Health in Boston. "The worry is we're raising a generation of kids in front of screens whose brains are going to be wired differently."

What to do? Give those brains some rest! "Recent imaging studies," the *Times* report said, "have found that major cross sections of the brain become surprisingly active during downtime. These brain studies suggest to researchers that periods of rest are critical in allowing the brain to synthesize information, make connections between ideas, and even develop the sense of self."

"Bring back boredom!" says Rich, who gave a speech in October to the American Academy of Pediatrics called "Finding Huck Finn: Reclaiming Childhood from the River of Electronic Screens."

I never thought I'd hear an educator put in a good word for boredom. But I salute the Harvard professor. So should everybody in the business of creating new ideas or rethinking old ones: writers, artists, composers, scientists, inventors, reformers. Some of our most creative work gets done in downtime—waking from a nap, taking a walk, daydreaming in the shower. (Writers are particularly clean.) Downtime is when breakthrough ideas are delivered to us, unsummoned, when yesterday's blockages somehow come unblocked. That's because we treated ourselves to a little boredom and cleared our brains of the sludge of information. Try it.

E-Maledictions

IT'S A LIFE CHOICE: I DON'T HAVE EMAIL

I'M STRUCK BY how many people chastise me for not using email. It's as if I have violated the order of the universe. My decision doesn't seem strange to me. It's the result of certain choices I've made about how I want to live my life. I meet a lot of people who are being driven crazy by their dogs, but I don't say, "Why do you have those stupid dogs?" They *like* being driven crazy by their dogs. It's a life choice.

I don't have email because I don't need it in my work and I don't want to be the captive of its daily clutter. I don't need group emails from organizations I belong to. I don't want to be sent jokes, good or bad, or recipes, or family vacation photographs, or solemn articles that the senders think would be my intellectual salvation, or books in progress by writers who want me to edit their work or find them an agent. I'm free! And it feels terrific.

My rebukers come in two categories. "Oh, you're one of *those*!" the first group says, visibly irked that I can't give them an email address. Others ask me how I can be such a Luddite. They think it's their moral obligation to scold me into the modern age. I'll admit that I'm a selective Luddite. I find much of the old technology easier to use than the new technology. Can anyone open a plastic-sealed package without power tools?

But I welcome any scientific advance that makes sense for me. Luddites don't write blogs. How can I not love a technology that gives me an on-line column every week to replace the readership I had in the now-dying world of print journalism. Yet that technology hasn't altered my lifelong intentions. I still believe in the carefully written personal essay, a long-esteemed literary form.

My other rebukers—a larger category—tell me how much I'm inconveniencing them. "You put me to a lot of trouble," one said. "I wanted to invite you to a book party, but you don't have email." That didn't strike me as a sequitur; I'm easily found in the Manhattan telephone directory. My friend was e-inviting his party list and didn't want to pick up the phone. Another friend said she wanted to send me something, but I didn't have email. Her tone suggested that I had entered a Trappist monastery.

"Put it in the mail," I told her. The mail! I could almost hear the neurons in her brain processing the successive hardships of finding an envelope, a stamp, and a mailbox.

"Oh, all right," she said, much aggrieved. "I'll send it by snail mail."

That's a term I really dislike. Snail mail is the United States Postal Service, a venerable organization of hardworking men and women who bring us our checks and bills and other clerical essentials, our magazines, our catalogues, and one of life's purest gifts—a personal letter.

Last week I received a letter that I wouldn't trade for a bushel of emails. It came from a woman I hadn't thought of since 1976. At that time I was master of Branford College at Yale, and Sara de Beer was one of its 400 students. But I still remembered her because she had an intense scholarly interest. She was in love with the idea of storytelling as an academic form, and we worked together to get a course established.

"I want you to know how grateful I am," she wrote in her letter last week, 35 years later. "You enthusiastically embraced my most absurd ideas and helped me bring them to fruition. Your encouragement and support continue to sustain me." She said she had searched my Website for an email address—in vain—and had necessarily taken up pen and paper. Forced to use an envelope, she had also enclosed a flyer describing her current work—as a professional storyteller ("Sara can design a storytelling event to meet your needs"). She had remained true to her girlhood dream.

What I did for Sara de Beer was nothing out of the ordinary. It's what teachers are put on earth to do: to help students grow into the people they are supposed to become. But most teachers never hear from their students again.

I treated Sara's letter like a sacred object and filed it with my papers, perhaps to be found by some future researcher with a dream of her own. If she had just sent me an email I don't think I would have handled it so tenderly.

4

Faraway Places

The Last of the Lone Wanderers
WHAT ELEVATES TRAVEL WRITING
TO LITERATURE

IN 1933 AN 18-year-old Englishman with a literary bent
and a nomad's turn of mind, Patrick Leigh Fermor, set out
to walk from the Hook of Holland to Constantinople. Two
years later he arrived. Even on foot that's a long time to
get between two points in Europe. But the hiker stopped
to talk—and often to stay—with everyone he met. They
were the oddest of odd lots of races and religions and
tribes. Some were members of defunct Danube royalty—
barons living in ornate Transylvanian castles with large
eclectic libraries. Some were Hungarian gypsies, some
were Romanian shepherds, some were monks. High or
low, they offered hospitality to the English visitor and told
him strange and often amazing stories. I think they were
grateful that someone had made an effort to find them in
their remote villages and valleys and to wonder who in the
world they all were.

Long afterward, Leigh Fermor would reconstruct that
odyssey in two books, *A Time of Gifts* (1977) and *Between
the Woods and the Water* (1986), that became minor travel
classics, much loved for their erudite, observant style. He
was the last of Britain's great solitaries—men and women
who sought out harsh and inaccessible places—and his
death two weeks ago at the age of 96 closes the door on a
remarkable body of travel literature.

The region that called out powerfully to those "desert eccentrics" was Arabia, luring them to superhuman

feats of endurance and assimilation, especially Charles Doughty, Richard Burton, Freya Stark, T. E. Lawrence, and Wilfred Thesiger. Doughty's monumental *Travels in Arabia Deserta* (1888) remains the masterpiece of the genre, exhaustive in its cultural detail.

But it is Sir Richard Burton, as always, who captures our imagination. The glamorous explorer of the source of the Nile, who knew 24 European, Asian, and African languages, smuggled himself into the holy city of Medina, garbed as an Arab, and then into Mecca, in 1853, during the Hajj. How he accomplished that perilous feat, first immersing himself in intricate Arab rituals of dress and etiquette, is vividly told in *Personal Narrative of a Pilgrimage to Al-Madinah and Meccah* (1855).

Freya Stark was the first Western woman to travel through the Arabian deserts, and her many books about those trips—including *The Southern Gates of Arabia* and *Riding to the Tigris*—are models of the travel essay form. "She has a genius for traveling on her own," one critic wrote. "It is the unexpected that brings out the best in her."

T. E. Lawrence, another brilliant loner, wandered through the Middle East before World War I as an archeological snoop—a warm-up, as it turned out, for leading the Arab revolt in the desert. His classic book about that campaign, *Seven Pillars of Wisdom*, is both an adventure yarn and a meditation on Lawrence's many enigmatic obsessions.

Wilfred Thesiger was the first white man to cross the dreaded "empty quarter" of Arabia, and in *The Last Nomad* he describes that journey—an excruciating tale of heat, thirst, and deprivation that he seems to have hugely enjoyed.

The last practicing member of the breed was Bruce Chatwin, whose *In Patagonia* (1977), a book of surprising stories about reputed mythical beasts and other legendary oddities, took him across the wild southern tip of South America. In a subsequent book, *The Songlines* (1987), Chatwin went still farther off, to northern Australia, where he traced the paths—heard but not seen—by which the aboriginal people sang their way from one destination to another. It now occurs to me that nothing so gladdened the heart of an English solitary as a place that had no roads.

One of those English wanderers indirectly crossed my own path. In 1944, I was a GI in North Africa, intoxicated by a culture dramatically different from my own and eager to learn more about it. But I assumed that no books had been written in English that would answer my traveler's questions. Then one day a book came in the mail from my mother—*Fountains in the Sand* by Norman Douglas, an account of his walk across Tunisia in 1912. Just from its chapter titles—"By the Oued Baiesh," "The Stones of Gafsa," "The Gardens of Nefta"—I knew that the book would fill my need for a predecessor in this unknown land. Douglas was famous mainly for *South Wind*, a novel set on an island easily recognizable as Capri. But I know him best for his solitary walks to corners of the Mediterranean so plain and primitive—*Old Calabria* is typical—that it takes a certain perversity to want to go there.

The worlds that those restless hermits wrote about were often interior worlds, tinged with mysticism, and it could hardly be otherwise; they achieved their destiny by following trails that weren't on any map. But what raises travel writing to literature is not what the writer brings to a place, but what the place draws out of the writer. It helps to be a little crazy.

The Old Flotilla

CHECKING OUT KIPLING'S BURMA

On the road to Mandalay,
Where the flyin'-fishes play
An' the dawn comes up like thunder
    outer China 'crost the Bay!

RUDYARD KIPLING's maudlin poem, sung by generations of voice-proud baritones, has foisted on the world some curious notions of Burmese topography, starting with the bay across which the dawn comes up outer China. No such China-facing bay exists; no flying fishes play on the road to Mandalay.

I'm not saying Kipling was fact-challenged; he was, after all, born in Bombay. He just needed some *ay* words to rhyme with Mandalay, and God forgives poets stuck for a rhyme. But what about that old flotilla that so euphoniously lay?

Come you back to Mandalay,
Where the old flotilla lay:
Can't you 'ear their paddles chunkin' . . .

I always liked that beautiful line and wondered what it could possibly mean. A few years ago I found out.

In 2004 my wife, Caroline, and I decided to celebrate our 50th wedding anniversary with a trip to Burma. We had first gone there half a century earlier, in 1955, and had greatly liked the Burmese people. But the military government had restricted our stay to five days in and around Rangoon. Strictly forbidden were the sites we most wanted to see, farther up the Irrawaddy River, the 1,000-mile highway that runs down the center of the country: the old royal capital of Mandalay; the vast plain of 2,000 ancient pagodas at Pagan; and the villages of the ethnic tribes in the north and in the Shan State to the east. Our dream would have to wait.

Five decades came and went, and successive juntas kept the nation, which they renamed Myanmar, mostly shut. Then, one day in 2004, a travel brochure came in the mail announcing a 17-day tour of Burma that would start with a six-day voyage down the Irrawaddy. I could hardly believe the alignment of destinations and dates. The trip would cover all the places we had been waiting so long to see and would begin exactly on the 50th anniversary of the day we were married in the First Presbyterian Church of Cedar Rapids, Iowa.

Our boat, the brochure explained, was a newly built replica of the flat-bottomed paddlewheel steamers that once were the lifeline of the towns and villages along the Irrawaddy. That fleet of 650 boats, an astonishing creation of the British Empire, which annexed Burma in three wars between 1824 and 1885 and ruled it as a colony until 1948, was built by a Glasgow shipyard, founded in 1865, called the Irrawaddy Flotilla Company. The Irrawaddy Flotilla Company! When the Japanese invaded Burma in 1942, the British sank more than 600 of the boats to deny them to the enemy, and today the flotilla survives only as a line in a poem by Rudyard Kipling.

Our group assembled in Rangoon, and we flew north to the market town of Bhamo, near the Chinese border, where the *Pandaw II* was waiting for us by the riverbank. It looked like a giant shoebox—a longitudinal edifice with no pretense of nautical grace. But the interior was elegant: polished teak decks, shiny brass fittings, and handsome rattan furniture. Outside our stateroom, two rattan chairs invited us to put our feet up on the railing and watch the Irrawaddy go by—which I endlessly did.

One of our first stops was at the logging town of Katha, where, in the 1920s, George Orwell discontentedly served with the British colonial police—a period he would evoke in his novel *Burmese Days*. We hiked into the jungle to watch a team of elephants—remnants of the legendary labor force long employed in the teak forests of Burma and northern Thailand—working the logs of a teak station not unlike the one that Orwell's protagonist supervised.

Many of the villages where we went ashore were seldom visited by tourists and had a harmonious serenity. Sometimes I would detach myself from our group and just sit in a village and enjoy the fact that I was there. I didn't have a single noun or verb in common with the men and women and children whose lives I had dropped into, but they always made me feel welcome and safe, inviting me to sit among them or bringing me under a thatch roof if one of Burma's instant rainstorms caught us by surprise. I was totally contented. New York boy goes Buddhist.

But some part of my mind was also out on the river, where I heard a distant chunkin' of paddles and a faraway hammering of nails in a Scottish shipyard blessed with the most musical of all corporate names: the Irrawaddy Flotilla Company. Today it would be IFC.

At Home in the South Seas

LOOKING FOR JAMES NORMAN HALL
AND ROBERT LOUIS STEVENSON
IN TAHITI AND SAMOA

THE BLOCKBUSTER TRILOGY *Mutiny on the Bounty* was written by James Norman Hall and Charles Nordhoff in the 1930s in Tahiti, where both men had their home. Hall's widow, Sarah Hall, still lived in the house that she and her husband built 10 miles outside the town of Papeete, and in 1956, on a writing tour of the South Seas, Caroline and I went around to see her.

It was a comfortable wooden house with spacious rooms and screened verandas that looked out on garish tropical foliage. Hall had been dead for five years, but he was still alive in the house, his hat hanging on a peg, his typewriter and a falling-apart atlas waiting on an ink-stained blotter, his thousands of books spilling into the kitchen. That library included 27 volumes by Joseph Conrad, who was Hall's hero and for whom he named his son. (The cinematographer Conrad Hall would win an Academy Award for *Butch Cassidy and the Sundance Kid*.)

Keeping Joseph Conrad company were the complete works of Robert Louis Stevenson, the 12-volume *Works of Benjamin Franklin*, the nine-volume *Writings of Thomas Jefferson*, and sets of Washington Irving, Thoreau, Emerson, Hawthorne, Mark Twain, Thackeray, and Sir Walter Scott. Modern American literature was broadly represented: Thurber, Steinbeck, Sinclair Lewis, Sarah Orne Jewett, and the writer Hall most admired, Willa Cather. One entire wall was crammed with works of naval history: *The Life of Admiral Bligh, Trial of the Bounty Mutineers, Sea*

Life in Nelson's Time by John Masefield, *English Seamen* by Robert Southey; 60 volumes of the *Annual Register* of England from 1758 to 1857; and countless other reference volumes, some with place markings sticking out and notes scribbled in the margins.

"I was always jealous of the books—they took so much of my husband's time," Sarah Hall told us. "He once asked me what I wanted to do with them when he died—maybe give them to a library? I said, 'Why, Jimmy, it wouldn't be my house if it didn't have those books.'"

Today I sometimes think of that library, assembled on a faraway speck of land by an American boy from Colfax, Iowa (population 1,749), because no such library will ever be assembled again. The world's knowledge has been digitized, its literature is fast being Kindled. Does any architect still design a house with a "library"?

Book-lined rooms were part of our shared domestic landscape. To walk into a house with books was an unspoken promise of conversation that would jump beyond the events of the day.

From Tahiti we went to Western Samoa, staying at Aggie Grey's Hotel, a ramshackle boarding house that was an iconic destination for traders and beachcombers—and writers—roaming the islands of the South Seas.

Samoa's other famous landmark was a ménage of high respectability. Poised on a hillside just outside town, "Vailima" was the house that Stevenson built in 1890 for his extended family from Scotland—including his mother and wife and stepson, the writer Lloyd Osbourne—where he would spend the last four years of his life. He had come to the South Seas in search of a benign climate for his tuberculosis and sailed widely among the islands, which first beckoned him as a boy in Scotland. The Samoans called him "Tusitala," teller of tales, and when he died in 1894, at the age of 44, they carried his coffin to the top of the small mountain that rose out of his garden, where he wished to be buried. In a clearing at the summit—probably the most inaccessible grave in English letters—the teller of tales lies beneath a simple stone inscribed with the epitaph he wrote for himself:

Under the wide and starry sky
Dig the grave and let me lie
Glad did I live and gladly die
And I laid me down with a will
This be the verse you grave for me
Here he lies where he longed to be
Home is the sailor home from the sea
And the hunter home from the hill

"Vailima" was an agreeable white frame house with several verandas and broad views down to the Pacific. Some Samoans thought Stevenson's ghost lived in the house, but we only felt serene vibrations there, and so did G. R. Powles, the New Zealand high commissioner, whose official residence it was. Western Samoa was then a New Zealand trust territory.

"Mrs. Powles and I have lived here for eight years," he told me, "and we're alone at night—the servants sleep out. But never once have I snapped awake in the dark and thought, 'What was that?' as you do in so many houses." I couldn't help thinking of all the boys who stayed up late reading *Treasure Island* or *Kidnapped* or *Dr. Jekyll and Mr. Hyde* and later snapped awake thinking, "What was that?"

On the Trail of the *Chêng Ho*

FROM CORAL GABLES, FLORIDA,
TO A HARBOR IN TAHITI

OF ALL THE travel books on my shelves, faithful remind-
ers of places I once traveled far to see, one that often tugs at
me is *Garden Islands of the Great East: Collecting Seeds from
the Philippines and Netherlands India in the Junk "Chêng
Ho,"* by David Fairchild. That's a book I'm highly unlikely
to own; botany is a subject I've never been accused of boring my friends with. Yet if I open Fairchild's 1943 book to
its endpapers, I see a map of the voyage he made in 1940
through the Moluccas, the old Spice Islands of the Dutch
East Indies, to gather plants for what would become the
Fairchild Tropical Gardens in Coral Gables, Florida. Tracing his route, I can still smell the copra boat I took through
those same Moluccas in 1953, and I think with gratitude
of the writer who sent me there.

S. J. Perelman was a licensed humorist practicing his
trade when the editor of *Holiday* magazine, Ted Patrick,
who elevated the craft of travel writing in the years after
World War II, sent him on two trips around the world. The
articles that Perelman wrote became the books *Westward
Ha!* and *The Swiss Family Perelman.* Those two trips made
a serious traveler of Perelman. He fell in love with Southeast Asia and talked knowledgeably about the region, his
famously esoteric vocabulary now seasoned with Malay
words and British colonialisms.

He fondly recalled taking a copra boat of the Dutch
K.P.M. line that "hemstitched" its way around the island
of Celebes, and he urged me to make the trip. He and I

were fellow addicts; travel, not writing, was what we usually talked about. I duly booked passage on a K.P.M. boat out of Macassar, and except for a choleric Dutch captain the trip lived up to Perelman's promise. I took along some names of helpful people he had met in the islands.

One was a Dutch planter named Daan Hubrecht. He told me he knew the Moluccas because as a younger man he had been a member of David Fairchild's plant-gathering expedition aboard "a junk called the *Chêng Ho*." The expedition was financed, he said, by an American explorer and science patron, Anne Archbold, who had the junk specially built in Hong Kong with a modern botanical laboratory below decks. Modeled on a 15th-century Chinese junk, it was brightly painted and decorated and was altogether, Daan Hubrecht said, quite a sight.

That junk stuck in my mind, and when I got home I tracked down a copy of *Garden Islands of the Great East*, Fairchild's account of the expedition. From its first paragraph I was hooked:

> It was sometime in the 1880s that [the naturalist] Alfred Russel Wallace came to the college in Kansas where my father was president and delivered a lecture on Natural Selection. I was too young to understand what Wallace said on the platform, but I listened intently to his conversation in our house the evening after the lecture. I like to imagine that it was this meeting with the great naturalist which started my longing to see, when I grew up, those islands of the Great East.

What attracted me was the idea of a boy too young to understand the lecture but not too young to recognize the lecturer as the model for his own life's work. By the time

David Fairchild went plant-gathering in the Moluccas he was an old man himself; the jacket photograph shows a white-haired gent standing on the deck of the *Chêng Ho*, holding a tray of what look like large round nuts. As always, his wife, Marian, who was the daughter of Alexander Graham Bell, went along on the trip. So did Anne Archbold.

After reading the book, I realized that *Garden Islands of the Great East* had its genesis on that night in the 1880s when Alfred Russel Wallace came to Kansas to lecture on natural selection. If there is one work that David Fairchild's book resembles in its lively scientific curiosity it is Wallace's mighty 1869 classic, *The Malay Archipelago*. It was in those same "garden islands" that Wallace, laboring independently of Charles Darwin half a world away in London, developed an almost identical theory of evolution.

The Fairchild expedition was halted after six months by the outbreak of World War II, but the descendants of the species it collected in 1940 are still alive and well in the Fairchild Tropical Gardens in Coral Gables. The book doesn't mention what became of the *Chêng Ho*.

In 1956 I spent a few weeks in Tahiti, and one day, at the far end of the harbor of Papeete, I noticed what appeared to be a derelict junk, pulled high up on the beach. Tahiti's capital was then a small town, and everyone who hung around the waterfront—the town's main occupation—knew everything about the inter-island boats that were the connecting tissue of the South Pacific.

I asked if anyone knew about the junk. Everyone did. They said it was called the *Chêng Ho*, and it had led a succession of picturesque lives during World War II, serving as, among other things, a radar ship and a naval officers' club in Honolulu. After the war it fell into private hands and was occasionally sighted in various ports of the South Seas, finally coming to rest in Tahiti.

There was more to the story than any one teller of tales had pieced together, and for a while I thought of pursuing it myself; the *Honolulu Star* was said to have an extensive file. In the end, however, I let the scent grow cold.

Tristes Tropiques

WHEN SCREENWRITER ERNEST LEHMAN
REPAIRED, VERY BRIEFLY, TO TAHITI

ONE DAY IN the fall of 1956 my wife and I were waiting on a dock in Suva, the capital of Fiji, to board a flying boat to Tahiti. No other air service to that island paradise was then available; the seaplane that was to drop us in Tahiti wouldn't come back for two weeks.

Among the waiting passengers I noticed a slight American man in his late 30s who looked tremendously alone. I introduced myself and he said he was Ernest Lehman, a screenwriter from Hollywood. At that time I was the movie critic of the *New York Herald Tribune*, and I asked Ernie what movies he had written that I might have reviewed. To my relief he mentioned *Somebody Up There Likes Me*, a boxing film starring Paul Newman, which I had recently seen and liked.

I asked Ernie why he was going to Tahiti. He said, "To get away from it all." I asked what the "all" was that he was getting away from, and it all came spilling out. He said he had just been hounded off the set of *Sweet Smell of Success*, the movie being made from his *Cosmopolitan* magazine novella, by its producers, Burt Lancaster and Harold Hecht. Lancaster also starred in the movie as a venomous Broadway gossip columnist.

But the filming had unleashed a Waterloo of egos that I could only guess at in Ernie's haggard face. He had been fired as screenwriter—replaced by Clifford Odets—and told to get lost. "We'll read the reviews over your grave, Ernie," Lancaster told him. Broken and exhausted, he was ripe for the getaway advice of a friend who spoke the magic word: *Tahiti*.

Like all the writers and dreamers who preceded us, Caroline and I were greatly taken by Tahiti's beauty and languor. But Ernie Lehman was deeply morose. We spent a lot of time trying to jolly him over travel's little surprises; he was a likable and humorous man. But even in the South Seas only so much can be done to cheer up an urban neurotic.

What finally undid Ernie was the absence of news from the outside world. In 1956 Tahiti had no newspaper or radio station; nobody knew or wanted to know what was happening anywhere else. Two of the major events of the postwar era—the Suez war and the Hungarian uprising—took place during our stay. We didn't know about either one.

But for Ernie the deprivation was harsh. One day he happened to mention that his hobby was ham radio; he had a shortwave tower behind his house in Brentwood, and he talked about the pleasure of hearing faraway voices across vast distances late at night. That evening we looked for him at our hotel and couldn't find him.

The next day he turned up for breakfast in a high mood. He had spent the day trying to locate a shortwave radio operator and had finally heard of a Frenchman who lived in the mountains. He hired a taxi to drive him up there, and he implored the Frenchman to make contact with someone in Los Angeles. Fiddling with his dials until well after midnight, the Frenchman had almost lost hope when Ernie heard the faint crackle of a familiar voice.

"It was Mel Shavelson!" Ernie told us. Shavelson was a screenwriter whose name I had often seen on amiable comedies like *The Seven Little Foys*. "I arranged for a phone patch to be put through to Mel and we talked for half an hour," Ernie said, catching us up on the week's movie grosses and the latest studio chitchat. I was glad to see him so happy; I hoped Mel's fix would tide him over until the plane came back to get us.

But two days later a steamship put in at Papeete, heading east, and Ernie bought a ticket and was gone. At Panama he caught a flight to Los Angeles—never again, as far as I know, to leave. We followed his career with affection and visited him several times at the house with the shortwave tower.

Ernest Lehman would long outlive Hecht and Lancaster and his other tormentors—he died in 2005 at the age of 89—and would become one of Hollywood's most successful screenwriters. *North by Northwest* is a classic original, a model of urbanity and wit, and *The Sound of Music* is the third-biggest-grossing film at the domestic box office. Some of his other films were *Executive Suite*, *Sabrina*, *West Side Story*, and *Who's Afraid of Virginia Woolf?* In 2001 he received a Lifetime Achievement Award from the Academy of Motion Picture Arts and Sciences—the first screenwriter so honored.

He would also know the satisfaction, not given to many writers, of seeing one of his phrases, "the sweet smell of success," ushered overnight into the American language.

At Ease in the Stone Age

CLOSING THE GAP BETWEEN
FINCHINGFIELD AND IRIAN JAYA

I THINK OF Norman Lewis as the best travel writer of our times, and in 1995, when a travel magazine asked me to go to England to interview him, I didn't lose any time getting on the plane. Lewis was then 87 and had just come home from a journey through three of the most hostile regions of Indonesia that concluded with a stay in a Stone Age village in the mountains of New Guinea. I wanted to catch him before he took off again.

I was introduced to Lewis's first two books—*A Dragon Apparent*, about Indo-China, and *Golden Earth*, about Burma—in the early 1950s, steered to them by his fierce admirer S. J. Perelman, another writer besotted with Southeast Asia. Trailing Lewis to remote jungle settlements where most travel writers would dearly love not to go, I found myself in the company of a man with all-seeing eyes and no regard for his own comfort or safety. He had a deep interest in indigenous peoples and their threatened way of life; a sense of imminent loss hovers over his work. He moved among those ethnic tribes with intuitive ease, often in moments of considerable danger. What kept him alive, I think, was a gift for finding amusement in the routine outlandishness of life, which drained the worst situations of their terror. That dry humor also runs through his writing style.

Now I was in the picture-postcard town of Finchingfield, an hour north of London, where Lewis had long lived—between trips—with his wife, Lesley. It was perfect English weather—rainy and cold—and their house was perfectly English in its lack of central heating. Lewis led me to the one room that he claimed had some heat, and we settled down to talk. After a few minutes he stood up. "I'm going to take my jacket off," he said. "It's frightfully hot in here. Do you feel too warm?" I assured him that I had never felt too warm in England.

Talking with this civilized man in the prim English countryside, I thought of the vast distance separating him from the aboriginal people he had befriended in the jungles of Asia and Latin America, and I wondered what qualities of mind had gone into closing that gap.

"I've found that in the whole gamut of society," Lewis said, "people have many similarities. Recently, when I was in a Stone Age village in Irian Jaya, I met a man who had learned a little English from the missionaries. I've noticed that when native people have close connections with white people, their faces start to change. As I looked at this man I could see the sharp-faced boy who lives in the East End of London, and I said, 'If I had come here 10 years ago, what would have happened to me?' He said, 'We would have eaten you.' But he knew it was funny, and we both laughed at that. That man is living more than 20,000 years back from you and me—back in the mists of the origin of mankind—and yet he had a recognizable sense of humor. And I knew he would. If you're in this profession a staggering number of years you gradually develop a set of muscles for these things. You have to, in order to survive. I practically know what people are thinking if I try very hard."

5

Language

Unexpected Visitors

"WHAT IS YOUR favorite word?"

That question came in the mail recently from an editor compiling a book in which various authors would name their favorite word and explain their reasons.

"I don't have a favorite word like *williwaw* that I keep in a display case to moon over," I wrote back. "Those words please me when I see (and hear) them, but unless they fill a precise need—*oscillate, lapidary, filigree*—I abstain, fearful of being sucked into the bog of academic prose where monsters like *adumbrate* and *ineluctable* lurk."

My favorites are the hundreds of vivid replacements for words that are just too dull—too *humdrum*—to make writing come alive. *Brazen,* used instead of *bold,* not only catches the reader off guard with the fanciful *z*; its sound exactly conveys its meaning. A brazen scheme is more than merely bold; listen and you'll hear a mountebank.

I write by ear, and sound is what leads me to what I'm rummaging for. In a column prompted by the death of the singalong host Mitch Miller, I explained that beneath his pop persona Miller was an erudite classical musician, not "a TV talk-show *pantaloon.*" Words with an *oo* sound—*voodoo, boondoggle, hooligan*—are irresistible in their playfulness. What a pleasure to throw *pantaloon* into my column and simultaneously define the genus talk-show host.

Surprise is the most refreshing commodity in nonfiction writing. Snoozing readers are startled awake to find that a writer is actually trying to entertain them. I strive for that moment. My style consists mainly of plain one-syllable and two-syllable words, but I'm always listening for the interloper from some distant corner of my education or my travels—not a word that's trying to be "fancy," but one that's doing precision work.

Here are three sentences from my book *Writing Places* that particularly pleased me when they finally fell into place:

> I was one of the first magazine writers to go to San Francisco in the winter of 1967 and bring back news of the "love hippies" who had descended on the Haight-Ashbury district, decked out in "ecstatic dress" and drugged out on LSD—flower children running away from their parents in the slumbering suburbs. I had no way of knowing I had climbed aboard a wave that would move at tsunami speed. By June it had washed a tide of ragged postulants to San Francisco, where they camped out for a "summer of love" that the city's health and safety officials hope never to see the likes of again.

Beyond the small felicities of alliteration and metaphor I really like *postulants*. I don't think I ever used it before, but it sprang from some recess of my brain when I needed a word to describe earnest young men and women seeking admission to a religious order. I like to find words from a specialized discipline—religion, medicine, music, carpentry—that I can put to use in a general context. In 2009, on the Sunday before the much-ballyhooed unveiling of the new Yankee Stadium and the Mets' new Citi Field, I wrote in the *New York Times*:

> I assume that the new stadiums will feature the latest advances in audio-visual assault. I stopped going to Mets

games at Shea Stadium when my friend Dick Smolens and I could no longer hear each other talk between innings—such was the din of amplified music and blather from the giant screen in center field. But baseball is also a game of silences. Every half-inning it invites its parishioners to meditate on what they have just seen and to recall other players they once saw play.

Parishioners, also borrowed from religion's vocabulary, specifically means a group of like-minded people assembled in a temple for a sacred ritual. Very satisfying. Here's one last dip into the liturgical soup. Recalling several magazine editors who kept me busy with writing assignments, I wrote: "Pamela Fiori, editor of *Town & Country*, which for a century had *catechized* its readers on the manners of the Eastern establishment, found me useful as her house WASP."

Medicine is particularly rich in terms begging to go out in public: all those words like *sclerosis* that doctors toss about so freely to inform us of some new clogging or erosion. *Sclerotic* is a perfect adjective for political punditry. Fifty years later I still remember a sentence by S. J. Perelman referring to the *peristaltic* prose of the columnist Max Lerner.

Obama and the Lac Bug

HERE'S HOPING OUR PRESIDENT GETS
MANY MORE SHELLACKINGS

I'M GLAD TO SEE 2010 depart because the newspapers will finally stop summarizing the year for me, wrapping it up in handy 10-packs. The 10 best books. The 10 best movies. The 10 best everything else. Now can we please get on with living our lives?

One recent list, in the *New York Times*, was devoted to words or phrases that entered the language in 2010. One word was *refudiate*, courtesy of Sarah Palin. Another was *vuvuzela*, the South African plastic trumpet that whacked the eardrums of spectators at the World Cup matches in Johannesburg. Some of the new usages (*retweet*) were born of new technology. Some (*containment dome*) washed ashore with the Gulf oil spill; some (*put-backs*) crawled up from the sewer of mortgage foreclosure. *Enhanced pat-down* was a gift from Homeland Security.

But I was puzzled to see *shellacking* on the list of new arrivals, prompted by President Obama's comment that he took "a shellacking" in the 2010 midterm elections. As a synonym for defeat, *shellacking* has long been a sportswriters' darling, and as for its root word, *shellac*, I first heard it when I was barely out of the crib.

My great-grandfather Wilhelm Zinszer, who came to New York City as a young man in the great German emigration of 1849, had been foreman of a shellac factory in Mainz, the center of the German furniture industry, which depends on shellac to coat and finish its products. Americanizing his name, he founded William Zinsser & Company and built a small shellac factory and a small house far "uptown" at what is now 10th Avenue and 59th Street. I have a photograph of those two buildings, alone in a field sloping down to the Hudson River; the only visible form of life is a goat.

The business stayed on that block for 125 years, finally moving to New Jersey in 1975 when progress forced it off its hillside. Even in 1954, when my wife entered the family and was shown around the factory by my father, she couldn't believe that such a Dickensian agglomeration of pipes and vats still existed in industrial America.

But the end product of all those pipes got our family through the Depression and would put my three sisters and me through college. At an early age we knew the life cycle of the lac bug, which secretes a resinous cocoon onto the twigs of trees north of Calcutta, and we could recite the many wonderful uses of that insect's resin. Shellac famously went into phonograph records. Shellac gave stiffness to playing cards and felt hats. Depression-era families stayed home and listened to a lot of records and played a lot of cards, and every American man wore a fedora—even when he was standing in a breadline, as photographs of that period poignantly remind us. Because shellac is a natural substance, unlike varnish, it could be swallowed without harm and was therefore used to coat pharmaceutical pills.

In its second generation, William Zinsser & Company faltered, and my father left college in 1909 to rescue it. A born merchant who loved his business, he built it into the position of leadership in the industry that it has occupied ever since, the name ZINSSER calling out to customers from the shelves of every hardware store. I often meet people who recognize my name and can't wait to tell me about the blissful afternoon they spent refinishing their basement with a shellac-based Zinsser product.

Although I was the only son, I didn't go into the business, my ready-made future, but followed my own dream to become a newspaperman. My father gave me his blessing and recruited a son-in-law to replace me, and the firm was finally sold out of the family in 1986. But I've never stopped feeling its residual tug. I still get messages on my answering machine left by homeowners seeking product advice.

I've never known how the benign *shellac* became the fierce *shellacking*, lodged in the headline writer's lexicon of verbs signifying the many gradations of humiliating loss: *vanquish, drub, rip, rout, thump, thrash, trounce, pummel, wallop*. I don't buy that usage for President Obama and his administration. I'm a big Obama fan, and I hope he gets many shellackings in the years ahead. I want him to be coated and protected from all the nicks and scrapes of adversity, his leadership sealed against the harsh winds of contumely by the lowly lac bug.

Literate Revelry

LIGHT VERSE GETS NO RESPECT

WHEN I BECAME a Harper author, in the 1950s, the firm occupied a red brick building, five stories high, at Park Avenue and 33rd Street. On its façade a sign in italic gold letters said *Harper & Bros., est. 1817*. It was the kind of building where you felt you could walk in and actually see an editor at work, possibly one who had been with the firm since 1817.

Today the company is housed in the innards of a high-security tower in midtown Manhattan and has undergone many mergers and mutations. I have variously been a Harper & Bros. author, a Harper & Row author, and a HarperCollins author. At one point in this fluctuating history the company held a party for my longtime editor

Buz Wyeth to honor him for his 35 years of service with Harper—a rare act of fealty in an industry where editors hop from nest to nest like migratory birds. The then-head-honcho of the company invited me to the party and asked me to "say a few words" about Buz.

Something about the way he said "a few words" made me think he meant it, and I decided on the format of light verse, limiting myself to the sonnet length of 14 lines. The problem would be to find 13 rhymes for Wyeth, but for us light-verse junkies that's the kind of puzzle that makes the world go round. Here are my few words for Buz:

> When the writer's talent drieth,
> Peters out and petrifieth,
> When ol' writer's block denyeth
> Inspiration and he sigheth,
> Sleepeth late and alibieth,
> Moaneth low and me-oh-myeth,
> Whimpereth and why-oh-whyeth,
> Lieth down and like-to-dieth,
> David daunted by Goliath,
> Then whose wisdom most applyeth
> When the gadding muse gadflyeth?
> Where's the balm that satisfyeth?
> What's the Buz word that he cryeth?
> "Let me die—or get me Wyeth!"

Light verse gets no respect as a literary form. Some would say it's not even a literary form. Some might even spell it lite verse. Today America is crosshatched with poetry workshops and MFA poetry programs, and I think I can safely bet that the words *light verse* will not be found in their descriptive literature.

But I've always enjoyed the form—and so, I suspect, have a lot of other people, nursing their guilty secret in the privacy of their homes. At weddings and birthday parties and anniversaries I'm repeatedly struck by the outpouring of light verse in toasts and congratulatory speeches, much of it remarkably good. As a form it's anything but easy, requiring nimble feats of compression, allusion, exactitude, and wit.

Mainly, however, I like light verse because its purpose is to amuse, and that seems to me to be a good day's work. Edward Lear's nonsense poems are a serious contribution to the world's enjoyment, much loved for their playfulness, and many American writers—Ogden Nash, Phyllis McGinley, E. B. White, John Updike, Calvin Trillin— wrote light verse that conveyed their pleasure in entertaining both themselves and their readers. Trillin still does.

It consoles me to remember that the form did have one golden moment. During the late 1920s and early '30s, all of New York's newspapers carried a daily column of light verse, most famously Franklin P. Adams's "The Conning Tower" and Don Marquis's "The Sun Dial." They encouraged submissions from their readers, and it was in those hospitable columns that many men and women who later made their name as writers and playwrights and wits— Dorothy Parker, Russel Crouse, Dorothy Fields, Alexander Woollcott, Robert Benchley—first saw their name in print. As E. Y. (Yip) Harburg put it, "We lived in an age of literate revelry in the New York daily press, and we wanted to be part of it."

No Proverbs, Please

WRITING ENGLISH AS A SECOND LANGUAGE

TWO AUGUSTS AGO I gave a talk about writing to the incoming class of foreign students at the Columbia Graduate School of Journalism. They were roughly 80 young men and women, newly arrived from a multitude of countries—Bhutan, Ethiopia, Sierra Leone, Thailand, Uzbekistan—about to be plunged into the harsh reality of writing clearly and comfortably in a language very different from their own. I knew the magnitude of that task; I tutored many of their predecessors in previous classes at the journalism school, trying to ease them over the shoals of bewildering syntax, linear narrative construction, and high anxiety. In my talk I wanted to tell the new crop of foreign students what problems they would encounter.

I began by posing a question: "What is good writing?" It depends, I said, on what country we're from. We all know what's "good writing" in our own country. We grow up immersed in the cadences and sentence structure of the language we were born into, so we think, "That's prob ably what every country considers good writing. They just use different words."

I once asked a student from Cairo, "What kind of language is Arabic?" I was trying to put myself into her mental process of switching from Arabic to English. She said, "It's all adjectives." Well, of course it's not all adjectives, but I knew what she meant: it's decorative, it's ornate, it's intentionally pleasing.

Another Egyptian student, when I asked him about Arabic, said, "It's all proverbs. We talk in proverbs. People

say things like 'What you are seeking is also seeking you.'"
He pointed out that Arabic is full of courtesy and defer-
ence, some of which is rooted in fear of the government.
"You never know who's listening," he said, "so it doesn't
hurt to be polite. Don't forget—we go back to the pha-
raohs." That's when I realized that when foreign students
come to me with a language problem it is often a cultural
or a political problem.

I think it's lovely that such a decorative language as
Arabic exists; I wish I could walk around New York and
hear people talking in proverbs. But all those adjectives
and all that decoration would be the ruin of a journalist
trying to write in plain English about the events and issues
of the day.

Spanish also comes with a heavy load of beautiful baggage that would smother a journalist writing in English.
The Spanish language is a national treasure, justly prized
by Spanish-speaking people. But what makes it a national
treasure is its long sentences and melodious long nouns
that express a general idea. Those nouns are rich in emo-
tion, but they have no action in them—no people doing
something that we can picture—something that we ourselves might do. Aspiring journalists from Spanish-speaking countries must be given the bad news that all those
long abstract sentences will have to be cruelly chopped
up into short sentences with short nouns and active verbs
that drive the narrative forward. "Good writing" in Spanish is not necessarily "good writing" in English.

So what is good English? It's not as musical as Spanish or Italian or French, or as ornamental as Arabic, or as
vibrant as some of the other languages that the foreign stu-

dents at Columbia grew up with. But I'm hopelessly in love with English because it's plain and it's strong. It has a huge vocabulary of words that have a precise shade of meaning; there's no subject, however technical or complex, that can't be made clear to the ordinary reader in good English. If it's used right. But that's a longer story, and in the rest of my talk I tried to tell it.

Yes, But

I COLLECT SELF-CANCELING HEADLINES,
BUT I'M TIRED OF THEM

I'VE BECOME A collector of a new journalistic form, commonly found in the news sections of the *New York Times*. It's the self-canceling headline. The top line states a fact or a situation; the second line starts with *But* and says, in effect, "It won't work."

GOP LISTS SWEEPING GOALS,
BUT THEIR IMPACT IS UNCERTAIN
Translation: No need to read this. Come back next year.

CITY NOTES DIP IN CRIME,
BUT WORST VIOLENCE IS UP
Translation: You won't get robbed, but you may get killed.

Even when the headline doesn't contain *But*, the message is no less apocalyptic.

ELECTIONS AROUSE HOPE
AND DOUBTS IN MYANMAR

AS HEALTH LAW
SPURS MERGERS,
RISKS ARE SEEN

Risks are seen, fears stoked, losses predicted. Also de-lays and obstacles, setbacks and snags. Questions linger. Misgivings are expressed. Legislators balk. Naysayers say nay. It's a lexicon for the faint of heart.

I started my collection last summer after a bout of eye surgery left me temporarily unable to read small newspaper type. Instead I just scanned the headlines and found myself living in a world that had come to a standstill.

HOSPITALS MAKE NO HEADWAY
IN CURBING ERRORS, STUDY SAYS
Translation: It's still not safe to get sick.

EVEN REUSABLE GROCERY BAGS
CAN CARRY ENVIRONMENTAL RISK
Translation: Don't bother going green. Nothing can
    be done about this stuff anyway.

MANY STENT PROCEDURES,
THEN MULTIPLE LAWSUITS
Translation: Have you been thanking God for the stent
    that saved your husband's life? Not so fast!

We can be glad that the giants of American history weren't deterred by the headlines in the morning paper.

JEFFERSON WRITES 'DECLARATION,'
BUT BRITS VOW ARMS BUILD-UP

LINCOLN FREES SLAVES,
BUT REBS SEE BLOODSHED

I'm not a *but* person. I'm a *probably* person. I think bold ideas can be made to work if enough people believe in them. America was built by *but*-ignorers. Quite a few of them were women: Susan B. Anthony, Eleanor Roosevelt, Rosa Parks. Many were inventors and scientists: Wilbur and Orville Wright, Henry Ford, Jonas Salk. Some were athletes: Jackie Robinson, Roberto Clemente. Some were just mavericks with a crazy dream. Gutzon Borglum proved in the hills of South Dakota that even an immigrant's son could move mountains.

My eyes are better now, so I could go back to reading the actual articles in the *Times*, not just the headlines.

But doubts remain.

Prisoners of Britspeak

THE ELOCUTION PROBLEM
WITH ENGLISH MOVIES

MY WIFE AND I got some good news the other day: we aren't the only people who can't understand British actors. Until now we have nursed our shameful secret in the privacy of our apartment, hunched over the television set, watching English movies that we would probably enjoy if we could unlock the strangled syllables.

We first realized the severity of our problem in 1984, when PBS unveiled a lavish miniseries, *The Jewel in the Crown*, based on Paul Scott's *The Raj Quartet*, four intertwined novels about the twilight of British colonial rule in India in the early years of World War II. The thing about quartets is that they have a lot of characters, all carrying the accumulated baggage of previous liaisons and umbrages, and Paul Scott amply filled that quota, providing the usual rapes, false accusations, shootings, deaths in childbirth, racial defamations, and stifled homosexuality. Dozens of picturesque men and women came and went, discussing those entanglements, and the people they were addressing seemed to know what they were talking about. We weren't so lucky. Quite often we would ask each other, "Did you understand any of that?" Are you kidding?

The good news we recently received came from the drama critic of the *New York Times*, Ben Brantley, in his review of a revival of Tom Stoppard's play *Arcadia*. "Some of the performances from the Anglo-American cast," he wrote, "are pitched to the point of incoherence in those nasal passages where upper-class twangs are thought to dwell." Hallelujah! Somebody out there *understands*. "Unless an emergency diction coach is brought in," Brantley said, "I suggest you read *Arcadia* before seeing it this time."

That's not really the point of going to the theater. The point of going to the theater . . . well, you know what it is. It's to *hear* the play. By the nature of his job the *Times* drama critic has heard hundreds of hours of Britspeak, and if *he* needs an emergency diction coach I feel better about the disability that afflicts our household.

By now we've learned not to rely for our evening's entertainment on a British movie that gets a star in the TV listings. The film begins, and we give it our best attention, grateful for plausible behavior in a sea of New Jersey housewives and dog whisperers. We also owe it to our so-called common heritage; my mother's forebears were English and my wife's were Scotch. But after a few minutes we begin to list toward the TV set, ears straining to catch the swallowed vowels. Soon it occurs to us that this is harder work than it ought to be. Corrective words are spoken: "Shall we see what's on *Law & Order*?"

I'm struck by how many British males narrate "important" American television programs. Their voices are presumed to confer on the show a gravity not found in the American larynx. How often have I been vocally escorted through a *Nova* special—riddles of the sphinx! mysteries of the brain!—in Oxford tones of grim authority. How often have I been jollied up some Himalayan mountain with hearty chin-up fortitude by a British male leading an expedition to find long-lost Bhutanese tombs.

What really annoys me is when a Brit is chosen to narrate a deeply American subject. I once tuned in to a TV special on the history of jazz and heard a titled English voice explaining the genius of Louis Armstrong and Charlie Parker. His tone was proud and avuncular, as if Armstrong and Parker had grown up on the docks in Cheapside or maybe in the Cotswolds. Hey, guys, the river that jazz came up was the Mississippi, not the Thames.

Fantasia for the Left Hand

REHABILITATION POETRY FOR
A WOUNDED FRIEND

CORPORAL RICHARD MOHR came into my life in the fall of 1945. World War II was long over, but we were still stuck in the Army, waiting at a camp near Naples for a promised troopship to come one day and finally bring us all home. Time passed slowly. But Dick Mohr had many time-passing talents. One was Ping-Pong. He had been a teenage Ping-Pong hustler, and that sport killed many hours in the servicemen's club. I couldn't believe how many of my unreturnable shots got returned.

He was also a bibliophile. Sometimes we would hitch a ride into Naples and he would go book hunting. His collector's nose led down narrow Neapolitan streets to antiquarian bookstores that had somehow survived in the bombed and broken city. Poking among long-forgotten volumes on long-unvisited shelves, he would find one or two books that had rarity or scholarly importance, which he would buy and send home to his parents in Indianapolis.

He was also a demon typist. One day he extracted from the base commander a two-day pass—for himself and for me—in exchange for typing a tortuous military document with superhuman speed and accuracy. Dick also insisted on the loan of a jeep, and he whisked us off to Sorrento, the town longingly invoked in the song heard in every Italian restaurant. I never forgot that my miniholiday overlooking the Bay of Naples was bought by my friend's typewriter.

After the war, married and settled in Los Angeles, Dick and his wife, Martha, founded and operated from their basement a business called International Bookfinders. Those years were a golden age of library building in America. Big state universities, especially the University of Texas, tired of not being Harvard or Yale, spent lavish sums to acquire valuable collections of books and manuscripts, and Dick knew how to gratify their dreams. He would systematically buy books that he could later form into collections around a particular author or theme. Lubricating his success were the descriptive catalogues that he wrote and typed. He was a man totally happy in his work.

In his early sixties Dick had a cerebral episode that impaired the use of his left hand. Afterward his wife gave me a list of the letters on the left-hand side of the typewriter. She asked me if I could arrange them into words that Dick might use as a recovery exercise. They were an unpromising lot, missing three of the five vowels—*i, o,* and *u*—and including *q, x,* and *z*.

I managed to quarry almost 250 words out of Martha's list, and I sent them to Dick. But they were dismal words—no fun for a man who had been nourished by the felicities of language. Therapy could only work, I felt, if it contained an element of enjoyment.

I remembered that Maurice Ravel composed his *Piano Concerto for the Left Hand* at the request of the concert pianist Paul Wittgenstein, who lost his right arm during World War I as a soldier in the Austrian army. A brother of the philosopher Ludwig Wittgenstein, Paul used Ravel's concerto, which is still in the classical repertory, to rebuild his smashed career. Later he also commissioned pieces for the left hand by Benjamin Britten, Paul Hindemith, Sergei Prokofiev, and Richard Strauss.

Inspired by that sinister body of work, I wrote my own left-hand opus—rehabilitation poetry—for my own wounded friend:

Fantasia for the Left Hand

crazed zebras craved egress
at a garage
scared bats vacated

a wet sweater starts a stagger
devastates a swagger

vexed rex
deferred sex
rested testes

ragtag beggars
degraded a revered settee
a reefer dazed a referee

drab cad
dabbed at a cravat
bad dad
treed a deaf cat

a fezzed Arab
razzed a verger
at Qatar

retarded gaffer basted a stag
braggart ate a garbage bag

saxes reverberate
cabbages vegetate
axes wax

aged drag star
segregated a sextet

exaggerated breeze
ravaged trees
wafted bees
afar

Dick Mohr never fully recovered. But my verses helped
to keep us connected and amused a little longer.

Flunking Description

WHY I TRIED TO WRITE LIKE A
VICTORIAN NOVELIST

I DON'T ENJOY descriptive writing; I was fed too much George Eliot and Thomas Hardy in school. I can take just so much heath and bracken. I also don't like to write what I don't like to read, so I reduce my sentences to the minimum number of facts I think a reader would want to know. Readers curious to learn more about what my people look like, or what they are wearing, or what they are eating, will remain curious. There will be no sentences like: "'I always wanted to be an actress,' she told me over a lunch of arugula tossed with balsamic vinaigrette, Stilton cheese, and a glass of Sancerre."

But in 2008, when I wrote a book called *Writing Places*, which was about the many odd sites where my caravan has stopped, I vowed to do better. A book grounded in the working habitats of a lifelong journalist should at least try— it wouldn't kill me—to paint a picture of what those places looked like. So I embarked on my Victorian journey.

My first job was at the *New York Herald Tribune*, and I dutifully described the glorious squalor of its newsroom: "Decades of use by people not known for fastidious habits had given the room a patina of grime. The desks were shoved against each other and were scarred from cigarette burns and mottled with the stains of coffee spilled from a thousand cardboard cups."

Venturing out into the paper's urban neighborhood, I recalled the exquisite seediness of Times Square, where, as the paper's movie critic,

I spent hundreds of hours in smoky screening rooms and then walked back to the *Trib* building past shooting galleries and X-rated movie arcades and novelty shops, past papaya juice stands and Nedick's and Bickford's, past strip clubs and jazz clubs and cheap hotels, past Jack Dempsey's and the Latin Quarter and the Paramount, where legions of bobbysoxers lined up on the sidewalk for a chance to swoon over Frank Sinatra, and, finally, past the horror-crazed Rialto Theater, at Seventh Avenue and 42nd Street, which beckoned me with ghoulish posters of monster movies and vampire movies, their titles dripping with blood.

That paragraph left me exhausted, and, as things turned out, it would be the book's longest chunk of description. In another chapter I recalled the flat in London where I wrote a profile for *Life* of the newly ascendant movie star Peter Sellers, "my Olivetti perched on a table obviously meant for teacups, my thoughts derailed every morning by a 'daily' who came to clean and stayed to talk in a Cockney accent too clotted to disentangle." That was it; nothing else came to mind that would interest me or anyone else. It now occurs to me that any British novelist would devote an entire page just to the displaced teacups.

Elsewhere in the book I described the shed in Connecticut where I wrote *On Writing Well* during the summer of 1974, a wooden outbuilding at the rear edge of our property, next to some woods, that the original family had built in 1916 as a garage: dirt floor, four walls, and a roof. It looked just big enough to hold a 1916-model car. I got a contractor to raise the shed onto cinderblocks, install a plywood floor and a few windows, and run an electrical line from the main house, enabling a light bulb to be suspended from a cord. I put my Underwood typewriter and its green metal table under the light bulb, along with a chair, a wire waste basket, a ream of yellow copy paper, and my *Webster's*. A wooden table completed the amenities. Later I bought a large fan; the office became fiercely hot by midafternoon, often requiring me to knock off for a compensating dip in Long Island Sound, which was as cold as the office was hot. Even the jellyfish stayed away until August.

So much for the office where *On Writing Well* was born.

In the 1970s, moving to Yale as a teacher, I was plunged into "a landscape of fortresses, their lineage descended from the castles and country estates of England, adorned with towers and turrets and moats and gargoyles and gates—a Gothic Disneyland." When I became master of Branford College at Yale I was not glad to find that my office was directly under Harkness Tower's 44-bell carillon:

> Probably I had heard the carillon from a distance as I walked across the campus and thought of it as mere perfume in the academic air. But that was from a distance. Now, overhead, the giant bells were less euphonious, their tone cloudy and not quite musical. They were also very loud. Nor was there much of a repertory for those bells. Occasionally one of the student carillonneurs, striving for relevance, played a Beatles song, but I don't think John Lennon would have taken it as a favor.

Of course there was more to be said about what it was like for our family to live in that moated fortress with 400 students, but that was anecdote and social history; no further description needed.

Still, as the book grew, its manuscript pages rising impressively, I was proud of my labors; I told myself I was really *writing*. But when *Writing Places* came off the press it was a very small book—small in size and weight and only 192 pages long. It wouldn't dent the stomach of anyone reading it in bed.

Yet it said everything I wanted to say about my lifelong journey as a writer and a teacher. I didn't turn into Thackeray after all. I flunked description.

Sharing the Issues

LET ME TELL YOU WHAT I THINK ABOUT THAT

"I HAVE WEATHER issues," my grandson told me several years ago, referring to the violent windstorm he had been caught in, which, for the rest of the summer, caused him anxiety when an even remotely dark cloud appeared on the horizon. He was seven years old.

Today in America nobody is too young to have issues. Toddlers have sandbox issues. Issues are what used to be called the routine hills and bumps of getting from morning to night. They have been around a long time; Job had issues. By calling them issues we wrap ourselves in the palliative language of therapy. We no longer phone or visit friends who are in trouble; we reach out to them. That way we can find closure.

And don't get me started on "share," the word I most loathe in the feel-good lexicon. I first learned in the 1970s that "share" really means "dump on." As master of Branford College at Yale, I dreaded the approach of any student counselors who said, "May I share something with you?" They seemed unduly pleased to be bearing some morsel of dishevelment that I, the sharee, didn't really need to know. Since then "share" has crept into popular usage as a synonym for "tell." "Did Rick share with you that we're coming for dinner tonight?" He did. He told me.

A heap of sharing was perpetrated after the recent death of the reclusive writer J. D. Salinger, especially in the pages of the magazine that was his mother church, where several staff writers retroactively outed the hermit of Cornish by sharing what a sociable guy he was if you only knew him. The important thing about Salinger is that he was a writer, just as Thoreau was a writer when he moved to a cabin at Walden Pond because he "wished to live deliberately." I doubt if the local townsfolk lost much sleep over how Henry was coping with his issues during the two years he spent in the woods. Living deliberately, he learned how to write one of America's sacred texts.

The "A" Word

WHAT'S EXPECTED OF AN ORTHODOX WASP

I WAS BORN into the Northeastern WASP establishment and have never quite stopped pretending that I wasn't. One word in particular has always dogged me unpleasantly. My parents both had charm and humor. In short, they were attractive. Their house was attractive and everything in it was attractive. That was the point of being a WASP: to be attractive. The laws were coded into my metabolism at an early age. Gaudy clothes and flashy cars were out. Understatement was in. A sweater the color of oatmeal was as attractive as you could get. I was careful never to be seen in a green jacket or tan shoes, or to use the wrong terminology. I said "curtains," not "drapes." I said "rich," not "wealthy."

Still, attractive as I was, I hated the word. It was a marker of class boundaries. "Is he attractive?" or "Is she attractive?" my mother or my sisters would ask when I talked about someone I had met. "Why don't you ask if they're *interesting*? Or *smart*?" I would snap, crabby as an old socialist. But the word has never stopped following me around.

Nor has the incessant naming of names. When I run into my WASP friends I know I'll soon hear the tinkle of tribal connections.

"You'll never guess who I saw last week. Muffy Pratt! She knew your sister at Smith and her sister Moo-Moo was my roommate at Saint Tim's. Wasn't her brother Buz in your class at Deerfield?" Even if he was I don't admit it. I deny all knowledge of the people mentioned in those conversations.

I went to Princeton, another WASP cocoon, but left during World War II to enlist in the army. I had no desire to be an officer, and the army obliged me in that populist whim. As a GI in North Africa, I got my first exposure to "otherness"—the Arab world—and it entered my veins like a narcotic, making me a lifelong traveler to places like Timbuktu and Yemen and Java that weren't on anybody's Grand Tour. I also made friendships with men I would otherwise never meet. I spent an entire winter in a tent in

Italy with a housepainter from Toledo and a policeman from Jersey City.

Home from the war, I was expected to join my father in the 100-year-old family shellac business; I was his only son. Instead I listened to my boyhood dream and got a job with the *New York Herald Tribune*. At that time newspapermen were a somewhat disreputable social class; nobody actually *knew* any newspapermen. I liked being an outsider and have since enjoyed making my own luck as a lone cowboy, following my own journalistic trails.

And yet . . . Who am I kidding? My origins leak through every effort to conceal them. I look like an old WASP (horn-rimmed glasses) and I have the habits of an old WASP. I always wear a jacket and a tie in the city and on trains and planes. (The jacket comes from J. Press.) If I see a photograph in the newspaper of a businessman without a tie I just know I wouldn't want him handling my business. I always wear a hat. I have very few clothes. I don't own any electronic gadgetry except the computer that I write on. I drive what my wife calls "an incredibly self-effacing car." I'm punctual. I never make a scene in public. I write personal letters by hand.

I'm aware that WASPs are a dying class. They are the only ethnic minority that other Americans may safely deride. But I also know that no class has so deeply imprinted its values on the national character: honor, hard work, rectitude, public service. By today's standards of civic and corporate governance those values look good, and I'm proud to be associated with them.

Today I often recognize fellow WASPs of my generation on the sidewalks of New York, a city they no longer own. They are always "nicely" dressed—old men and women facing the day with vigor and good cheer, disregarding the infirmities of age as they hurry to their next hospital board meeting or school tutoring session or fundraiser for some underfunded worthy cause. There's something about them that's—well, attractive.

6

Reverberations

Life and Work

WHY PLUMBERS ARE GOOD
ROLE MODELS FOR WRITERS

"WHAT IS THERE in life if you do not work? There is only sensation, and there are only a few sensations—you cannot live on them. You can only live on work, by work, through work. How can you live with self-respect if you do not do things as well as lies in you?"

So said the opera diva Maria Callas in an interview that I clipped from the *London Observer* in 1970. Unlike Callas, I can't hit a high C. But on the subject of work she and I are buddies. I've never defined myself as a writer, or, God forbid, an author. I'm a person—someone who goes to work every morning, like the plumber or the television repairman, and who goes home at the end of the day to think about other things. I can't imagine not going to work as long as I can.

I've never been—perhaps to my shame—a citizen of writing. I don't belong to writers' organizations, or attend writers' talks and panels, or lunch with publishing potentates. I don't hang out with writers. Writers tend to be not as interesting as they think. What they mainly want to talk about is their own writing, and they also have a ton of grievances, their conversation quick to alight on the perfidy of publishers, the lassitude of editors and agents, and the myopia of critics who reviewed—or didn't review—their last book.

I'm a lone craftsman, not unlike a potter or a cabinetmaker, shaping and reshaping my materials to create an object that pleases *me*—nobody else—and when it's done I send it forth into the world. I don't have an agent. I never show my writing to other writers; their agenda is not my agenda. For the objective judgment and emotional support that every writer needs I depend on the individual editors of my books and magazine articles—fellow craftsmen—and on a few trusted friends.

Many younger writers have taken me as a mentor, and when they come to New York they drop in for a checkup. Far too often I find them dispirited and professionally adrift, worn down by the glacial machinery of trying to get published: waiting for the phone call that doesn't get returned and for the check that isn't in the mail and for the decision on a manuscript that the publisher can't find ("I've been traveling a lot lately and I guess it got put in the wrong pile"), revising their article yet again for yet another editor who knows a great angle to satisfy the "marketing people," as did the two previous editors, now gone to other jobs without letting their authors know. Writers are one of nature's most insecure species; they shouldn't be in thrall to an industry so dysfunctional and discourteous. They should be writing what *they* want to write, not what their handlers tell them to write.

I try to refocus my frazzled writers on the *process* of writing, not the product. If the process is sound, the product will take care of itself. Recently I got a letter from a young woman writer who was back home in California after her annual visit. She said, "Your office is a sanctuary of craft amidst the hullabaloo of publishers, editors, and agents. You have no idea how liberating that is."

It may seem perverse that I compare my writing to plumbing, an occupation not regarded as high-end. But to me all work is equally honorable, all crafts an astonishment when they are performed with skill and self-respect. Just as I go to work every day with my tools, which are words, the plumber arrives with his kit of wrenches and washers, and afterward the pipes have been so adroitly fitted together that they don't leak. I don't want any of my sentences to leak. The fact that someone can make water come out of a faucet on the 10th floor strikes me as a feat no less remarkable than the construction of a clear declarative sentence.

No Degrees of Separation

LETTING GO WHEN THE KID
LEAVES FOR COLLEGE

OUR OLDEST GRANDCHILD is going off to college next week, and his mother, like mothers in every corner of the land, is contending with a lot of pain. How did time so suddenly accelerate? During the long journey of parenthood it often seems that the day when the first child leaves for college is so far off that it will never arrive. Then, one day, it does.

But the mother of our grandson will not go into the parting moment unsupported. His college has scheduled a full day of orientation talks, conspicuously including sessions of separation counseling for the parents, who otherwise might never leave. Those sessions are called "Letting Go."

Letting go is not a trait commonly associated with boomer moms and dads. Theirs is the generation for whom sociologists coined the term "helicopter parents"— a reference to their ceaseless hovering and whirring over the lives of their children. A growing number of colleges now offer a day of umbilical-cord-severing therapy. Parents are strictly required to be off campus by 5 P.M. On many campuses, however, they have been spotted several days later at the college's opening ceremony, sitting in the auditorium, still helicoptering.

Remember back when kids just got sent off to college? My Iowa wife, bound for her freshman year at Oberlin, where she had never set foot, caught a ride with some neighbors who were driving east and who dropped her off at her dormitory. At Oberlin, unimpeded by parental advice and visitation, she grew into the woman she was supposed to become and never looked back. Her parents got on with their lives.

When she and I later became parents I could hardly stand the thought of our daughter Amy going away to college. But remarkably soon she was home for Thanksgiving; I survived. I have no memory of driving her to college, and I only dimly recall visiting her two or three times, chatting with inscrutable roommates in cluttered student rooms. When our son John was at college we almost never telephoned him. If we did, his roommates invariably said, "He's at the library." We chose to believe it. Without our help he got an education that has since served him broadly as an artist and a teacher.

During the 1970s I was master of Branford College at Yale and could observe the annual arrival of our freshmen. What I saw were fathers performing labors that would make an actuary wince, lugging up many flights of stairs the possessions that their sons and daughters had brought to college to lubricate their education: hi-fi players, speakers, amplifiers, crates of LP records, books, posters, guitars, cellos, bicycles, house plants, waterbeds. (Today all the electronic gear could be carried upstairs in the palm of a hand.) Having discharged their historic function as porters, the parents were free to leave, and they soon did, administering separation counseling to each other on the drive home.

Except in emergencies I didn't see or hear from those parents again for four years, when, at commencement, I handed their children their diplomas. I had watched those long-ago freshmen stumble and pick themselves up and develop into interesting young men and women; that was the great satisfaction of the job. At the college we were left to play our traditional role of acting *in loco parentis*. The parents in turn took up their traditional role of creating interesting new lives of their own.

Today I wouldn't want the job. By definition *in loco parentis* means that the parents are somewhere else; they have left the *loco*. Now they are electronically present at all hours, peppering their children—and the college's administrators—with cell-phone calls, email messages, text messages, tweets, and cameo appearances on Facebook.

Hey, parents! Leave your kids alone! They're at the library.

Brother, Can You Spare a Job?

SONGWRITER YIP HARBURG
AND OCCUPY WALL STREET

THE BLACK CLOUD of unemployment hanging over the land got me thinking of the lyricist E. Y. (Yip) Harburg and his anthem of the Great Depression, "Brother, Can

You Spare a Dime?" It was written by Harburg and the composer Jay Gorney in 1932 for a musical, *Americana*, about "the forgotten man" and his betrayal by greedy capitalism. Gorney's stately minor-key melody, sung by a worker standing in a breadline, perfectly matched the dignity and the despair of Harburg's words:

> Once I built a railroad,
> Made it run,
> Made it race against time.
> Once I built a railroad,
> Now it's done.
> Brother, can you spare a dime?

The song so lacerated the national conscience that radio stations banned it; they said it was "sympathetic to the unemployed." But nothing could stop its momentum, especially after it was recorded by Bing Crosby. Overnight, "Brother, Can You Spare a Dime?" became the leitmotif of the Depression and a powerful goad to Roosevelt's New Deal. Today it still hovers in the national memory; I can hear its ghostly echo in the chants of the Occupy Wall Street marchers protesting the same inequalities.

Born Irwin Hochberg on New York's Lower East Side, Harburg never forgot the poverty of his upbringing or the toil of his immigrant parents in a garment industry sweatshop. Only Irving Berlin, another urchin of that Jewish ghetto, was born as poor. Almost all the other songwriters in that golden age of "The Great American Songbook" were children of bourgeois comfort. Richard Rodgers's father was a doctor. Jerome Kern, Lorenz Hart, Vincent Youmans, Burton Lane, and Alan Jay Lerner were the sons of prosperous businessmen. Harold Arlen's father was a respected cantor. Dorothy Fields's father was the popular comedian Lew Fields, and Oscar Hammerstein II came from a famous family of theatrical impresarios. They were also well educated. Cole Porter was a playboy who went to Yale. Rodgers, Hart, Hammerstein, Howard Dietz, and Arthur Schwartz went to Columbia, and Schwartz also had a law degree. So did Hoagy Carmichael.

But Harburg was not only an incurable socialist. He was an incurable dreamer. In 1939, with the composer Harold Arlen, he wrote the guileless score of America's favorite family movie, *The Wizard of Oz*, and its iconic ballad of infinite possibility, "Over the Rainbow." No lyricist was more temperamentally suited to imagine a kingdom where happy little bluebirds fly and troubles melt like lemon drops. Arlen called him "the lemon drop kid." An elfin man, known as Yipper, from *yipsl*, the Yiddish word for squirrel, he took Yip as his middle name.

But the squirrel never lost its political bite. In Harburg's 1944 Broadway musical *Bloomer Girl*, composed by Harold Arlen, the reform campaigns of the suffragette Amelia Bloomer gave the liberal lyricist such inflammatory themes as feminism and civil rights. Arlen wearied of Yip's insinuation of "propaganda" into the show and declined to work with him on *Finian's Rainbow*. The eventual composer of that hit show, Burton Lane, also demurred, hesitating for three months while trying to decide whether Harburg would drive him crazy. Harburg did. Although the lyricist was often at his whimsical best ("When I'm Not Near the Girl I Love, I Love the Girl I'm Near"), ultimately that fable of a crock of gold stolen from a leprechaun rested on the evils of capitalist materialism, which Harburg satirized in songs like "When the Idle Poor Become the Idle Rich." Afterward, Lane wouldn't speak to him for two years.

But the old socialist never stopped being true to what he believed, even when he was blacklisted by Hollywood for his political views during the McCarthyist 1950s. That was another distinction that set him apart from his fellow songwriters.

I've always resented messages in musicals and movies and other works of art. But as I watch the Occupy Wall Street movement struggling to be born, needing a Pete Seeger or a Bob Dylan to glorify its cause with a unifying anthem, I miss Yip Harburg and his nagging insistence that the American promise has gone badly askew. Until a new Harburg writes a new Depression rouser, here's a shot at adapting his old one:

Once I had an office,
Gave it juice,
Helped America throb.
Then the system busted,
Cut me loose,
Brother, can you spare a job?

Permission Givers

TO TEACH IS TO ALLOW
AND TO ENCOURAGE

WHEN RICHARD P. FEYNMAN, one of the giants of 20th-century physics, was awarded the Nobel Prize in 1965, he received hundreds of congratulatory letters from friends and admirers, including one from a former student named Koichi Mano. Acknowledging the letter, Feynman asked the young scientist what he was working on. Koichi sent a doleful reply, regretting that he wasn't working on fundamental problems of science, but only on "a humble and down-to-earth type of problem."

"Your letter made me unhappy," Feynman wrote back, "for you seem to be truly sad. No problem is too small or too trivial if we can really do something about it. It seemed that the influence of your teacher has been to give you a false idea of what are worthwhile problems." In his own career, Feynman pointed out, he had "worked on innumerable problems that you would call humble, but which I enjoyed and felt very good about because I sometimes could partially succeed." He went on to describe a dozen of those experiments, some of which failed, including one on the theory of turbulence that he "spent several years on without success."

I came upon this exchange in a book of letters to and from Feynman, published in 2005, called *Perfectly Reasonable Deviations from the Beaten Track*. Edited by his daughter, Michelle Feynman, the letters had languished for many years in 12 filing cabinets at the California Institute of Technology after her father's death in 1988. The ones she selected for this spacious volume are highly personal, most of them replying to "ordinary" people who wrote to Feynman with scientific questions. They are the letters of a born teacher.

Concluding his letter to Koichi Mano, Feynman wrote: "You say you are a nameless man. You are not to your wife and to your child. You will not long remain so to your immediate colleagues if you can answer their simple questions when they come into your office. You are not nameless to me. Do not remain nameless to yourself—it is too sad a way to be. Know your place in the world and evaluate yourself fairly, not in terms of the naïve ideals of your own youth, nor in terms of what you erroneously imagine our teacher's ideals are. Best of luck and happiness."

I'm a scientific rube, but I happened to become a Feynman watcher many years ago. I was attracted to his strong sense of enjoyment and to his engaging—and engaged—presence as a public man of science. Now, in these letters, I saw that he was also one of the great permission givers.

That's a type I'm always on the lookout for; permission is a scarce commodity in this land of multiple freedoms. I'm also in the permission business. As a teacher and as a mentor I give people permission to be who they want to be, and sometimes I think: How did *I* get stuck with this job? Isn't that what our schools are supposed to be doing? The answer, I've found, is that most Americans look back on their education as a permission-denying experience— a long trail of *don't*s and *can't*s and *shouldn't*s.

I've made that point in talks to college presidents and school administrators, and not one has ever argued back. All of them remember the prohibitions that were put in the path of their own advancement: the niggling caveats of dissertation committees, the envious gibes of peer reviewers, the dire threats that they will perish if they don't continue to publish.

Consider the American process of college admissions —a yearlong minuet of repudiation. *We dare you to get into our college! Your grades are excellent but not excellent enough. Furthermore, you don't play the oboe and you haven't spent any time digging wells in a village in Botswana.*

Writers! You must give *yourself* permission, by a daily act of will, to believe in your remembered truth. Do not remain nameless to yourself. Only you can turn on the switch; nobody is going to do it for you. Nobody gave George Gershwin permission to write "Rhapsody in Blue" at the age of 25, when he had only written 32-bar popular songs. Nobody gave Frank Lloyd Wright permission to design a round museum.

Sacred Objects

HALL OF FAMER EDD ROUSH'S LAST INTERVIEW

IN 1988, WHEN I went to Bradenton, Florida, to write a book about spring training, I learned that Edd Roush, the oldest living member of the Baseball Hall of Fame, had been a winter resident of the town for 36 years and was still a familiar presence at McKechnie Field, the Pittsburgh Pirates' winter ballpark, where he held court on a couch in left field and told everyone how much better the game was played in his day. He was 94 years old.

I thanked the journalistic gods who had delivered to my chosen town one of the game's authentic giants. From 1916 to 1931, playing center field for the Cincinnati Reds and the New York Giants, Edd Roush hit over .300 twelve times and hit over .350 in three straight seasons. Defensively, he ranks with Tris Speaker, Joe DiMaggio, and Willie Mays. He was famously cantankerous in his playing days, and time had evidently done no softening. Reporters on the *Bradenton Herald* warned me that he was particularly hostile to writers he felt were "pestering" him.

That didn't augur well for my getting an interview. Still, I was determined to try; no purer link to the National League's early days of glory would come my way, and time was running out. Not wanting to be rejected on the phone, I drove out to the house—a modest one-story dwelling on a small lot with two orange trees and a neatly lettered mailbox that said EDD J. ROUSH.

There was no doorbell—a deterrent to pesterers, I assumed—so I tried the kitchen door. After several minutes it was opened by a stern-looking older woman who said she was Mary Allen, Edd Roush's daughter. I explained my mission. She said she had heard about it. "Some damn fool from the newspaper called to say that a big writer from New York was in town to do a story about Edd Roush," she said. "There are three things my dad has no use for—preachers, teachers, and writers. That's why it took him until 1962 to get into the Hall of Fame. The baseball writers weren't about to vote for him. He had to wait until the old-timers committee voted him in. Of course he couldn't care less if he got in the Hall of Fame." She started to close the door. "We don't like to have writers sicced on us," she said.

Talking fast, I explained that I hadn't been sicced—that I was acting on my own. I was there mainly to pay my respects to Mr. Roush, I said, adding, however, that it didn't seem right for a book about baseball in Bradenton not to include her father.

Mary Allen looked at me long and hard through the screen door. Finally she turned around and I heard her say, "You might as well let him in, Dad. He's here anyway." She unlocked the screen door. "You can have 10 minutes," she said.

I think I expected to see a frail old man sunk into a sofa, probably wearing slippers. What I found was a small and very neat man sitting straight up in a chair. He was wearing a clean and pressed khaki shirt, a pair of clean and pressed khaki trousers, socks, and shined shoes. His hair was wet-brushed down, and he looked at me with vigilant blue eyes. Another damn-fool writer, they said.

I shook hands as ceremoniously as if I were meeting royalty—which I was. The hands and wrists were large— the hands of an Indiana farm boy, unreduced by age. They were the hands, I remembered, that had swung the heaviest bat ever used in major league baseball—48 ounces. I asked Edd Roush to tell me about the early days of spring training in Florida, and he recalled several ballparks that were little better than cow fields, full of holes. He described every nickel of his famous salary disputes with the tyrannical John McGraw—all of which he won. The blue eyes flared with the memory of outmaneuvering his old foe.

Mary Allen didn't kick me out when my 10 minutes were up, so I followed her into the kitchen and asked her about her own life. She said she had long been a schoolteacher in small Indiana towns. I mentioned that I had also done some teaching in Indiana, and soon it was as if there had never been a screen door between us. I asked Mrs. Allen if it was a burden to be a member of a Hall of Fame family.

"You wouldn't believe some of the stuff people send for my dad to autograph," she said. "Just last week the mailman brought a big box, and it was the slat of a seat from some stadium in New Jersey that got torn down. Well, there's no way Dad was going to sign *that*. We packed the thing up and sent it right back.

"Would you like to see what goes out of here in a typical day's mail?" she asked. I said I certainly would. We walked out to the mailbox, which she had stuffed with lumpy self-addressed packages containing baseball items that fans had sent to be autographed. I wrote down the destinations: East Petersburg, PA; Roanoke Rapids, NC; West Deal, NJ; Little Rock, AR; Center, MO; Canterbury, CT; Mahwah, NJ; Centralia, MO; Virginia Beach, VA; Bristol, TN; Brooklyn, NY.

Just then the mailman arrived. He took our oddly shaped packages and stuffed a new load into the mailbox. I looked to see what the day's tide had washed up: 12 envelopes from Idaho, Maine, and various states in between. The biggest—elaborately stamped DO NOT BEND— was from Forty Fort, PA.

I helped Mary Allen carry the packages into the kitchen, and then I went back and said goodbye to the oldest living member of the Baseball Hall of Fame. He was sitting straight up in his chair, staring fiercely into the past. Six days later Edd Roush died. He had a heart attack at McKechnie Field, just before a game between the Pirates and the Royals.

Today I still think of that Florida mailbox. For me it symbolizes a deep American yearning to connect with our idols through the artifacts of a shared passion. All those balls and bats and gloves that came back to the mailboxes of all the people who sent them were no longer mere balls and bats and gloves. Anointed by Edd Roush, they had become sacred objects.

Hats Off

AND THEN WHERE WILL
WE STOW THEM?

RELUCTANTLY BOWING TO fashion's timetable, I've put away my summer straw hat. It's a broad-brimmed Panama that far exceeds the uses expected of a hat. Most obviously, it covers my head. It also shields my eyes from the glaring sun. But mainly it gives me an identity in an age when men regard a formal hat as an object of fear and loathing. It's not that they don't put anything on their heads; they are swathed in all manner of caps and other strange contrivances. But those are not *hats*—attire befitting a walker in a great city. Last week on the subway I saw a Wall Street-bound man whose solemn black suit matched his solemn banker's visage. But on his head was an orange Phillies cap. That's someone seriously out of touch with the idea of fashion as an integrated statement.

In New York my straw hat stands out in a crowd because it's the only one in the crowd. "Yo, man! Love your hat!" bicycle messengers shout as they hurtle by. Women stop me say how "nice" I look in my hat and my jacket and tie. I thought that was the point of getting dressed to go to work: to look presentable and maybe to cheer up a few other people—a good day's work. Women have always known that; the sidewalk is their runway. "I love a good lid," the celebrity stylist June Ambrose told the Style section of the *New York Times* last week. "I like the punctuation of a hat. I like the drama."

Last year I was hailed on Fifth Avenue by the trendy fashion blogger Mister Mort. He loved my hat from half a block away, he told me, getting out his camera. He also loved my scarf and fussed over its threads as if they were rare jewels. My hat is the lubricant of my day. Storekeepers treat me seriously because my hat notifies them that I respect the city and the customer-merchant transaction.

There was a time when all American males, rich or poor, wore a felt fedora. Depression-era photographs remind us that every husband and father standing in a breadline—the ultimate indignity for a breadwinner—was wearing a fedora. So was every man watching a major league ballgame; pictures of Yankee Stadium and the Polo Grounds show a sea of fedoras. Gangsters in Hollywood movies were always sumptuously hatted, the bad guys looking even better than the good guys.

The chill of autumn has sent me out to find a new winter hat to replace my disintegrating Borsalino. The secret of a jaunty hat is a generous brim, but today's brims are so half-hearted that the quest has lost its fun. Last week I stopped at Saks Fifth Avenue and asked a clerk where I could find "men's hats." He gave me an odd look and a long pause. "Men's *hats*?" he asked. Finally he suggested that I try the sixth floor. I didn't know Saks even had a sixth floor. I took an elevator to that hat ghetto, gazed upon its paltry wares, and rode back down. Cross off another American institution: the hat department in your local department store.

Maybe that's just as well. Today a man with a hat can't even find any place to *put* it. I remember when every Broadway theater had a circular wire hat-holder attached to the underside of every seat. No such mercies survive. I've become a student of the generic coat closet in doctors' offices and other reception areas. I hang my outer coat in the closet and then survey the so-called hat shelf. Not an inch! Crammed into every last vacuum of space are rolls of toilet paper, mountains of paper towels, stacks of computer paper, bottles of Windex, and other unloved staples of office upkeep.

I proceed to the waiting room and sit on a chair with my hat on my lap, orphans from another age.

Peter McGuire's Holiday
SUMMER'S FINAL GIFT OF UNEXAMINED TIME

UNITED WE CROUCH like sprinters on the eve of Labor Day weekend, ready to hurl ourselves into the three-day swirl of activities required of every good American, squeezing the last ounce of pleasure out of summer's final gift of unexamined time. Officially, summer won't end for another three weeks. But in our bones we know that the jig is up. The new year begins next Tuesday.

On that morning we will wake to an altered landscape. Store counters previously heaped with bikinis and beach balls and suntan creams will be stacked high with three-ring notebooks. No mother can gaze upon those notebooks without a sinking of the heart. They announce that a new school year has arrived and that unspeakable related chores can no longer be postponed.

Cleaning out the children's closets. Yuck! Only the brave will wade into that midden of outgrown sneakers, torn T-shirts, broken flip-flops, and old issues of *Rolling Stone*. Once cleaned, those closets must be filled with back-to-school clothes. This is tricky terrain, as the shopping trip to the mall will soon reveal. Few areas of agreement exist between parent and adolescent on matters of age-appropriate wear.

Next come phone calls to the now-fully-booked dentist, orthodontist, and pediatrician. Then a mother turns to that other disaster area: the refrigerator. Gone is the season of the ad hoc meal, the cold cuts of July and August, the hastily assembled sandwich. It's time once again for real meals and dietary balance. It doesn't matter that the family has thrived for two months on food that a nutritionist might not call "food." A cycle has clicked, loud as the click from "wash" to "rinse." Out go the monster bags of potato chips, the giant jars of half-used mustard and ketchup and mayonnaise, the lemonade mix, the paper plates, the hot dog rolls with an encroaching patina of mold.

How did the nation get itself a holiday that holds such regulatory power over our lives? A day called Labor Day was first proposed in 1882 by Peter McGuire, general secretary of the United Brotherhood of Carpenters and Joiners of America. He felt that the country already had holidays to celebrate its religious, military, and civil traditions and that it needed one that was "representative of the industrial spirit—the great vital force of every nation." He suggested the first Monday of September because it fell roughly halfway between the Fourth of July and Thanksgiving. Twenty-three states gradually enacted the idea into law, and in 1894 Congress made it official.

McGuire's timing was perfect—he re-ordered the national metabolism. His day not only separates the languors of summer from the rigors of fall; it would generate many new social codes and customs. Young ladies were instructed that "Labor Day is the last day of the year when it is fashionable for women to wear white." Shoes, gloves, and handbags were pointedly included in that edict. Men: put away those shorts! Hirsute legs are no longer *de rigueur*.

But, above all, McGuire's holiday is a time of renewal. Next week the air will quicken with tidings of new life. New plays! New concerts and operas and ballets and art exhibitions! New TV shows! Season tickets! Benefits! The daily mail is a howling blizzard of charity extravaganzas. New cars! New sports: Football! Soccer!

Best of all, new friends—or, rather, old friends, finally back after their mysterious summer retreats. To a much-loved unreachable island off the coast of Maine. To flute camp. To Scrabble camp. To meditation camp. To Trollope camp. Whatever. But next week those migratory birds will return to the place where they belong. I'm grateful to Peter McGuire for yanking them home.

Great Moments with Mr. Lincoln

UP FROM DISNEYLAND, ON TO APPOMATTOX

ONCE, ON A VISIT to Disneyland, strolling along its strenuously quaint turn-of-the-century Main Street, past ice-cream parlors and candy palaces and penny arcades, I noticed a building called the Disneyland Opera House. On its marquee it said GREAT MOMENTS WITH MR. LINCOLN. I'm always up for great moments with Mr. Lincoln, and I went in to get a fix.

My fellow congregants and I were first shown a short film in which Walt Disney explained "Audio-Animatronics," the technology at the heart of his theme parks, enabling all manner of seemingly real people, animals, birds, and other critters to hail us as we come riding by. Disney said he first Audio-Animated Mr. Lincoln for the New York World's Fair of 1964, using a life mask taken in 1860, before Lincoln grew a beard. "The final result is so lifelike that you may find it hard to believe," the narrator said, and we were ushered into a theater to try to believe it.

The curtain went up and I saw a tall man in a black suit who somewhat resembled Abraham Lincoln. He was sitting in a chair, and something in me kept hoping he wouldn't try to get up. But he did, struggling arthritically to his feet and moving a few steps forward. He said he wanted to talk to us about liberty, and he expatiated on respect for duty, the law, faith in divine Providence, and dangers facing the nation. They sounded like disconnected homilies, and, as I later learned, they were—snippets from five speeches given during the mainly beardless years from 1838 to 1864.

This was not my writer's Lincoln. Was it anybody's Lincoln? As the tall man rambled on, emphasizing his points with hand and arm gestures that were angular and spasmodic, his long legs a little unsteady—would he *fall?*—I was reminded of another figure from the mists of Hollywood make-believe who moved with the same mechanical vulnerability, the same endearing wish to be human. It was Boris Karloff in *Frankenstein*.

That was a not-so-great moment with Mr. Lincoln. But otherwise my encounters with the 16th President always sustain me. He is the grave deity at the core of the American narrative, never far from my thoughts. I see him on my pennies and I see him on my stamps. I've seen him at Mount Rushmore, looking across the nation he preserved, and I've seen him in Washington, looking across the Mall where Martin Luther King Jr. sang his own song of emancipation. Above all I see him in his words. He is the writer I most often revisit to remind myself of the simple strength of the English language. His Second Inaugural Address, delivered only five weeks before his consuming war finally ended and six weeks before he himself was killed, is a sacred text.

One of my best moments with Mr. Lincoln took place at Appomattox. I knew that my book *American Places*, about 16 iconic sites, ought to include one Civil War landmark, but I didn't want it to be Gettysburg. I have no appetite for tramping across the battlefields of our saddest war, imagining the carnage and the military blunders that killed 620,000 men in four years. My Lincoln is a man of reconciliation. Instead the Civil War site I chose was not one where the armies fought but where they stopped fighting. Appomattox was both a longed-for end and a longed-for beginning; America could get on with the business of being a nation.

I flew to Richmond and drove west across southern Virginia, along the route covered by General Robert E. Lee during his last week with his 55,000-man army—a week that would end with his surrender to General Ulysses S. Grant, on April 9, 1865, in a tiny village that just happened to be handy when the dream of the Confederacy finally unraveled. Along the road I stopped to read a series of historical markers that told me how dire Lee's situation had become.

LEE'S RETREAT

SHERIDAN REACHED HERE ON APRIL 4, 1865, WITH THE CAVALRY AND WAS ENTRENCHED. HE WAS THUS SQUARELY ACROSS LEE'S LINE OF RETREAT TO DANVILLE. ON APRIL 5, GRANT AND MEADE ARRIVED FROM THE EAST WITH THE SECOND CORPS AND THE SIXTH CORPS.

Three days later it was all over. Outnumbered and almost encircled, Lee said, "There is nothing left for me to do but go and see General Grant, and I would rather die a thousand deaths." On April 9 he sent his aide into the village called Appomattox Court House to find a suitable place for the two men to meet. There, in the house of a merchant named Wilmer McLean, Lee asked Grant to write out the terms "under which you would receive the surrender of my army."

Grant took out a pencil, wrote rapidly at a small table, and handed the paper to Lee. The last of its four sentences gave the Confederate officers permission to keep their side arms and their private horses. "This will have a very happy effect on my army," Lee said after reading the terms, which, far from hounding the Southerners with reprisals, just let them all go home. Grant asked Lee if he had anything to add. Lee mentioned that the soldiers in his cavalry and artillery also owned their horses. Could those horses be kept? Grant agreed. He said he assumed that most of the men were small farmers and "because the country has been so raided by the two armies" he doubted that they could put in a crop to get through the next winter if they didn't take their horses home. "This will do much toward conciliating our people," Lee said.

More than a century later, through the stillness at Appomattox, that theme of clemency kept echoing in my ears. "Grant and Lee had to look far into the future," I was told by Ron Wilson, superintendent of the National Park Service site. "They knew that the energies that had been given to divisions for so many years would now have to be devoted to rebuilding the country. There was no vindictiveness."

Appomattox seemed to me to exist in a cul-de-sac of history, outside time, as if the village had been brought to life for just one event. Only three people were strongly alive to me. Lee and Grant continued to radiate powerful qualities that Americans still honor: one of them symbolizing the aristocratic tradition of the old South, the other personifying the self-made common man of the new North, Midwest, and West.

The third person was the inescapable Lincoln. Appomattox was, finally, his show. I could almost see him standing over the little table in McLean's parlor where Grant sat scribbling the surrender terms. As president, Lincoln had often spoken of wanting a merciful peace, but I didn't know if he and Grant had found time to discuss the situation, and I asked Ron Wilson when the two men had last met. He said they had met on March 27 and 28 at City Point—on the *River Queen* in the James River—and had talked at length about the approaching end of the war and the civil disorder it would bring.

"You just know," Wilson told me, "that Lincoln said, 'Let 'em down easy.'"

The Overtone Years
SYMPATHETIC VIBRATIONS AT THE AGE OF 89

THE NUMBER 88, referring to the number of keys on a piano, hovers in our collective memory. I remember a character in a Dick Tracy comic strip named 88 Keys, and I've listened to honky-tonk pianists who call themselves "Mister 88" or who "tickle the 88s."

As anyone who ever played a piano knows, the 88-note keyboard is our universe, bounded by the highest note that the ear can comfortably enjoy and the lowest note that a crazed Russian composer might compose. To venture beyond the wooden frame that encloses those 88 notes would be to fall off the earth.

Earlier this fall, if asked my age, I could say that I was just as old as the number of keys on a piano. Then, on October 7, I wasn't. I had outlived the standard Western keyboard and the largest piano. But then I was told that Bösendorfer, the Austrian manufacturer of sumptuous concert grands, makes a 9-foot, 6-inch model that has nine extra keys at the low end of the scale. I was saved! I had entered the Bösendorfer years.

Those nine extra bass notes almost never get played. But they give the piano a deeper and darker tone because their "strings," which are made of wire, are longer and thicker than the longest strings on a standard piano. They therefore generate overtones, which produce resonances with compatible notes of higher frequency farther up the scale.

So the Bösendorfer years are overtone years. That's as it should be—old age is mostly overtones. Older people have long since played all the necessary notes and musical forms: the joyful *capriccios* at the birth of a child or the graduation of a grandchild, the somber Bach fugues at the inevitable visits of disappointment and death. We are left only with the overtones of those long-gone events—their endlessly overlapping echoes and vibrations.

As a fourth-generation New Yorker, I live with overtones wherever I go. I pass the apartment where my parents lived to their own old age, and the *Herald Tribune* building where I had my first job, and the office where my wife came out of the Midwest to work for *Life*, and the various places where our children went to school and where we all went to church on Sunday. Those places send sympathetic ripples across the decades—intermingled memories of happy and productive times.

Today my city has been dimmed by glaucoma; the landscape is hazy. But my shoes still know the way. Every morning I walk from my apartment to my office, skirting long-familiar potholes and Con Edison excavations, and when I arrive I go to my computer, formerly an Underwood typewriter, as I always have. There I am anchored in my craft. The irrelevancies of the world close down around me and I'm alone with my materials, as the painter is finally alone with his canvas and the potter is alone with her wheel. I now write this column mainly from personal experience and remembered detail, not from external sources. I turn on my computer and I listen for overtones.

Acknowledgments

I WARMLY THANK Robert S. Wilson, editor of the *American Scholar*, for welcoming me to his website, and for his unfailing support and encouragement. I also thank his staff of careful and caring editors: Sandra Costich, Bruce Falconer, Margaret Foster, and Jean Stipicevic. They eased my two-year journey in a multitude of ways.

I thank Paul Dry, publisher of two of my earlier books, *American Places* and *Mitchell & Ruff*, and his editor, John Corenswet. Paul represents the best of independent publishing and is a loyal friend.

I thank John S. Rosenberg, my onetime student and longtime counselor, who again gave one of my projects its initial push.

Above all, I thank Allen Freeman and Caroline Zinsser, who were the editors of this book. I've never had two better editors.

Allen Freeman, advisory editor of the *American Scholar*, shepherded all 85 of my columns into electronic space. He was also my invaluable partner in matters of language, usage, tone, and musicality. He and I endlessly discussed shades of meaning. I entirely trusted his judgment.

Caroline Zinsser, my wife, nourished me with highly original ideas. She shaped the book with her intelligence and her love. The publishing adage was never more true: This book could not have been written without her.